ORCHIDS OF EUROPE

William Collins
An imprint of HarperCollins*Publishers*
1 London Bridge Street
London SE1 9GF

WilliamCollinsBooks.com

First published in the United Kingdom by William Collins in 2017

22 21 20 19 18 17
10 9 8 7 6 5 4 3 2 1

First published in Sweden by Bonnier Fakta 2017
Original title: *Orkidéer I Europa*
Copyright © 2017 Text Henrik Ærenlund Pedersen
Copyright © 2017 Illustrations Bo Mossberg

Design: Fredrika Siwe/siwedesign.se
Prepress: Mossart and Italgraf, Sweden
Print: Livonia Print, Latvia 2017

A catalogue record for this book is available from the British Library.

ISBN 978-0-00-821069-4

ORCHIDS
OF EUROPE

BO MOSSBERG & HENRIK ÆRENLUND PEDERSEN

WILLIAM
COLLINS

* CONTENTS *

How to learn more 197

Foreword

Amongst my earliest botanical acquisitions was a series of playing-card-sized illustrations of British orchids produced by the British Museum (Natural History) (now the Natural History Museum). These figured each species with details of its floral morphology highlighted and introduced me to the flowers growing on the chalk hills that surrounded our house in Brighton on the Sussex Downs. The highlight was always the Bee Orchid, a flower that epitomized my twin passions of insects and flowers. I am not alone in loving European orchids; they are perhaps the best-known and most charismatic flowers in the European flora.

The European orchid flora has been blessed with more studies than almost any other group of plants and has attracted botanists and amateurs in increasing numbers for over 200 years. Its literature is voluminous and varied; running from personal accounts and poetry to life-histories and field guides. Most of them are illustrated, historically by line drawings and watercolours but nowadays most frequently by colour photographs.

The majority of modern European orchid books are field guides. However, the fascinating life-history and ecology of orchids often receives scant attention in them. There is another tradition that looks in greater detail at orchids in the wild. A good example is Victor Summerhayes' *Wild Orchids of Britain* in the New Naturalist series (Collins, 1951, 2nd ed. 1968). The present fine work is much closer to Summerhayes' theme than to a conventional field guide. Both the beautiful illustrations and the text exhibit a detailed understanding of orchids acquired through long hours in the field over many years.

I am firmly of the opinion that good botanical illustrations will always have the edge over colour photographs. The artistic advantage allows an artist to depict hidden but significant details at a magnified scale, cover the life-story and seasonal variation in the plant and to place the plant in its typical surroundings. The best botanical artists combine all that with an inherent gift for design so that the product is both a thing of beauty and utility at the same time. Bo Mossberg's work is of the highest calibre, reminiscent of that of Raymond Piper who memorably illustrated the Irish orchid flora. This is surely a book that will broaden the understanding of our native orchids by those already hooked and will certainly inspire a new generation to a love and abiding interest in them.

Phillip Cribb
ROYAL BOTANIC GARDENS, KEW

Author's preface

M Y FIRST ENCOUNTER with native European orchids happened during an excursion with the Danish Ornithological Society to Öland, Sweden, in May 1980. On that trip, I enjoyed enormous populations of *Dactylorhiza sambucina* and *Orchis mascula* at peak flowering; and while the ornithologists were looking up to observe a pair of the rare Collared Flycatcher, I was down on my knees examining a young shoot of *Dactylorhiza maculata* ssp. *fuchsii.* I was hooked.

The orchid books illustrated by Bo Mossberg were some of the first I acquired while developing my new interest during the 1980s. Since then, my collection of orchid literature has grown considerably, but very few items (if any) have watercolours that equally well represent the natural appearance of the plants.

For the past 24 years, orchids have played a central role in my professional life. Besides involving field work in other continents, my orchid studies have taken me through major parts of Europe and given me opportunities to visit some of its most enchanting natural environments. Memorable experiences have included scenic helicopter flights in Lapland, getting stuck with a Land Rover in an Anglesey mire, handling a steadily growing pack of aggressive dogs in West Rhodopi and ending up on a ledge with cramping thighs after having lost my way on a steep wall in the Pindhos range. Orchid hunting may entice you into adventures of which you have never dreamt!

When I received Bo's invitation to compose the text for this book, it was a dream come true – more than 35 years after I first had the opportunity to admire his eminent work. It has been a great pleasure collaborating with Bo, and I sincerely hope that our joint efforts have resulted in a book that is capable of stimulating even more people to study, enjoy and care about these beautiful, fascinating and vulnerable plants. My own orchid studies have been continuously fuelled by inspiring input from numerous collaborators and travel companions over the years. I owe all of them my grateful thanks.

Henrik Æ. Pedersen
COPENHAGEN

*7

Illustrator's preface

ORK STARTED ON ILLUSTRATING the Nordic orchid flora in the mid-1960s. The first sketches were done on Öland, with the help of the local botanist Åke Lundqvist. This island, with its calcareous meadows and its mosses was the natural starting point for sketching orchids.

In the north of Sweden I made contact with the highly talented artist and botanist Rolf Lidberg and he guided me through his home territory. Rolf inspired me to continue painting orchids in southern and central Europe and was willing to accompany me on my trips to help me find orchids. Between 1976 and 1979 we travelled to places like Italy, Greece, Spain, Romania and the Crimea, resulting in the books *Nordens Orkidéer* and *Orkidéer: Europas Vildväxande Arter*, both written by the botanist and mycologist Sven Nilsson. These books were published by Wahlström & Widstrand and translated into several languages. The English translation, *Orchids of Northern Europe*, was published by Penguin Books in 1979.

The present book has a brand new layout and contains many new pictures; I would like to thank orchid experts Sven Hansson and Sven Birkedal for lending me photos that I have used in a number of close-up images.

The generic and specific names have been updated in accordance with Henrik Ærenlund Pedersen's naming system. His orchid research, scientific articles and books are pioneering. I am glad that he undertook the work on the texts for this book and I would like to take this opportunity to thank him for such a pleasant and rewarding collaboration.

Bo Mossberg
STOCKHOLM

Introduction

You ARE PROBABLY the proud owner of an orchid standing on the windowsill, and in that case you may already have noted some of the features characterizing the orchid flower. However, the improved orchids (mainly hybrids) that are being mass-propagated for retail only offer very limited insights into the diversity that exists among their relatives in the wild.

The orchid family (Orchidaceae), numbering some 25,000 species, is one of the world's two largest families of flowering plants. The vast majority of orchids are found in the wet tropics, and in those regions they exhibit an astonishing diversity in general appearance, structure, coloration patterns, floral scent, growth requirements, pollination mechanisms and so on. Only a minority produce flowers as large as those displayed on your windowsill, but many are true beauties *en miniature*.

Orchid systematics are being continuously studied and debated worldwide. In our view, Europe accommodates *c.*130 native orchid species partitioned among 33 genera from three subfamilies (for explanation of the systematic categories, see p. 16). Individual flowers are mostly small, but sometimes they are arranged in dense inflorescences of great beauty. Furthermore, the adaptations encountered in some of the European species are just as fascinating as those of their tropical relatives.

The present book provides an introduction to the native orchids of Europe. It falls into four main parts: 'Structure and systematics', 'Orchids and the environment', 'Orchid portraits' and 'How to learn more'.

Geographic coverage

For the purpose of this book, we have interpreted Europe in a traditional sense, largely adopted from the standard work *Flora Europaea* (Cambridge University Press, 1964–1980). Thus, our delimitation

Temporary work-room in Manfredonia, Italy

of European Russia and Kazakhstan to the east similarly follows the crest of the Ural Mountains and, further south, the Ural River to the Caspian Sea; and we, too, exclude the whole of the Caucasus. Furthermore, Cyprus and Anatolia are excluded, whereas Turkey north of the Sea of Marmara is covered. Outside Turkey and the former Soviet Union, all European countries are included in full. Thus, in contrast to *Flora Europaea*, we include Madeira, the Canary Islands and the East Aegean Islands of Greece.

Structure and systematics

In this part, we outline the overall characteristics of orchids, including both their underground and aerial vegetative organs and the structure of their flowers. We also introduce principles of classification and explain how scientific species names are composed.

Orchids and the environment

Under 'Orchids and the environment', the overall distributions and natural growth requirements of European orchids are characterized. Threats and conservation measures are briefly discussed, and we introduce the intimate relationships between orchids on the one hand and fungi and pollinating insects on the other.

Orchid portraits

This part constitutes the bulk of the book, and it presents all the individual genera in a sequence that is intended to reflect their most likely evolutionary relationships (to the limited extent that these can be translated into a linear sequence). In general, it means that genera being treated close to each other are mostly closely related.

Each genus is introduced by one page of text and illustrated by one or more colour plates on the following pages. The text consistently gives information on how to recognize the genus, where it is distributed, and the estimated number of species it contains – alongside information on the range of environmental requirements and flowering times in the European species. Depending on the genus, additional information may be found on topics such as pollination biology, associated fungi, evolutionary relationships or systematic problems.

The watercolours, supported by brief captions, illustrate the vast majority of European orchid species. For those species that are subdivided into subspecies or varieties (see p. 16), most of these are illustrated as well. To the extent possible, the sequence of species/subspecies/varieties (as represented by colour plates under each genus) follows the same overall principle as outlined above for genera.

How to learn more

The primary aim of this book is to prepare you for your first encounter with native orchids in the European countryside, but we decided to use the last part of the book to prepare you for the next steps. It gives you clues of how to improve your identification skills, how to organize field trips to other parts of the continent, and which societies and journals you can usefully consult to develop your network and knowledge base.

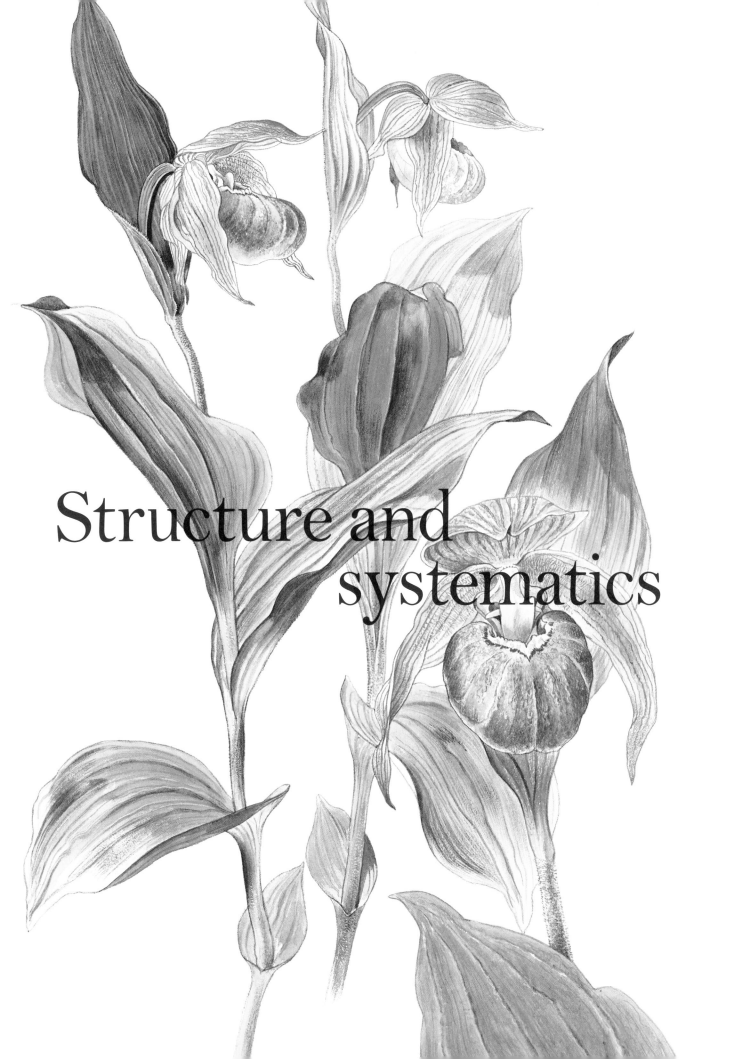

Structure and
systematics

The orchid plant

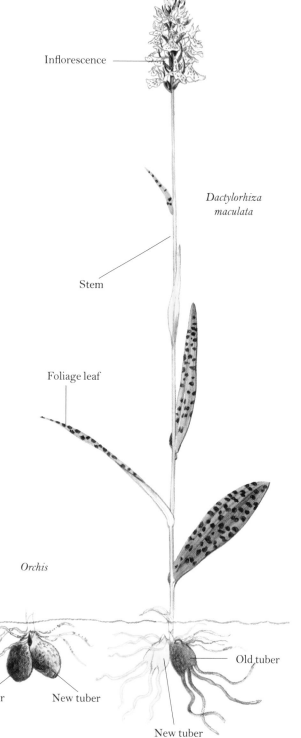

ALL ORCHIDS ARE PERENNIAL herbs. Most species grow as epiphytes (which means attached to trunks or branches of woody plants) in tropical forests. Epiphytic orchids often produce aerial roots, and many species store water and nourishment in freely exposed, swollen, bulb-like stems known as pseudobulbs. In contrast, all European orchids grow in soil (rarely bog moss).

Below ground

All European orchids store nourishment in short to elongated or coral-like underground stems (rhizomes), or in tubers that often combine root and stem tissue; a few species form underground pseudobulbs on a condensed rhizome. The vast majority of species produce roots, but these are sometimes few in number, and *Epipogium* and *Corallorhiza* have no roots at all.

　　Tubers, if present, are renewed annually. Thus, at the time of flowering, a tuberous plant will normally carry two tubers: a dark,

Inflorescence

Dactylorhiza maculata

Stem

Foliage leaf

Goodyera repens

Foliage leaf

Rhizome

Runner

Root

Orchis

Old tuber

New tuber

Old tuber

New tuber

partly shrivelled tuber from the preceding year and a new developing tuber that is pale and turgid. Vegetative propagation occurs when occasionally the old tuber is replaced by more than one new. In a few species, with or without tubers, vegetative propagation occurs by means of underground runners, and in yet other species the roots can form buds that develop into potentially flowering shoots.

Above ground

Aerial shoots consist of an unbranched, sometimes hairy stem bearing cataphylls (i.e. strongly reduced, basal leaves), foliage leaves and either a single flower or – much more commonly – several flowers that together form a terminal inflorescence. However, most species can also produce purely vegetative (i.e. non-flowering) aerial shoots.

The foliage leaves are normally well-developed and green, sometimes hairy and sometimes with brown or reddish-brown spots. When more foliage leaves are present, they are usually scattered on the stem or assembled in a basal rosette; in two *Neottia* species the only two leaves are placed opposite each other on the stem. In *Hammarbya*, vegetative reproduction occurs through the formation of tiny bodies, so-called bulbils, on the margins of foliage leaves; when the leaves decay during autumn, the bulbils are detached and may later develop into separate individuals.

In a few species, the foliage leaves are reduced to pale brownish sheaths or scales. In

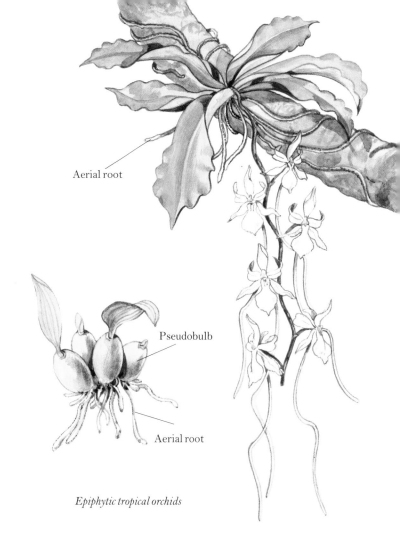

Aerial root

Pseudobulb

Aerial root

Epiphytic tropical orchids

such species, photosynthesis (the process by which green plants convert energy from sunlight to chemical energy stored in organic molecules) is absent or strongly reduced.

The inflorescence varies with regard to density and the number of flowers. Each flower is subtended by a small leaf, a so-called bract.

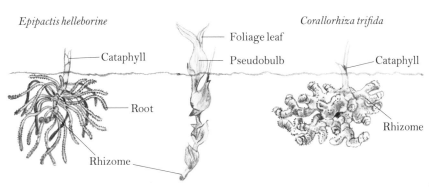

Epipactis helleborine

Cataphyll

Foliage leaf

Pseudobulb

Root

Rhizome

Corallorhiza trifida

Cataphyll

Rhizome

Hammarbya paludosa

The orchid flower

I N SPITE OF their great diversity of forms, all orchid flowers have nearly the same basic structure. To better understand this structure, it is useful first to observe a more familiar flower. For example, the flower of a Peruvian Lily has an outer and an inner whorl of three perianth leaves each – called sepals and petals, respectively. The female organs include an ovary (below the perianth) and a slender style that ends in a three-lobed stigma. Six stamens, free from the style, constitute the male organs; each combines a long filament and a terminal anther containing loose pollen. The orchid flower exhibits a few modifications of this structure.

Perianth

A highly characteristic feature of most orchid flowers is that the median petal is strikingly different from both the sepals and the lateral petals. It is usually of a different size and has a more complex shape. Because of its special nature, the median petal in orchids is referred to as the lip, whereas the term 'petal' generally is used only for the lateral petals. The lip often produces nectar in a concavity, sac or spur; but in some species the lip forms a spur without any nectar. In the flower bud, the lip is directed upwards; but in most species it is directed downwards in the open flower (usually due to 180° twisting of the ovary).

Sexual organs

The vast majority of orchids have lost all stamens but one, and the filament of this is fused with the style to form a 'column'. Two sterile rudimentary stamens may also be present. The pollen is united into two or four solid masses (pollinia) that sometimes have stalks. One or two adhesive bodies (viscidia),

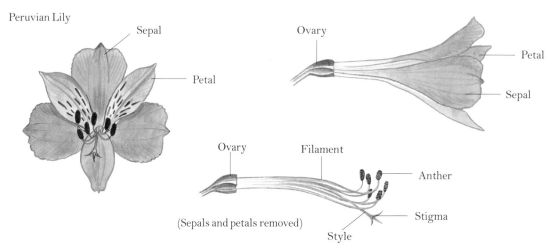

Peruvian Lily

Sepal

Petal

Ovary

Petal

Sepal

Ovary

Filament

Anther

Stigma

Style

(Sepals and petals removed)

Dactylorhiza maculata

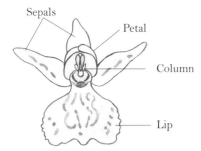

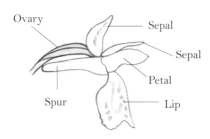

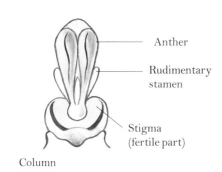

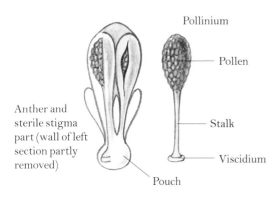

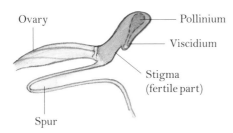

produced from a sterile part of the stigma, are attached to the base of the pollinia. The sterile stigma part may also form a barrier between the anther and the fertile stigma part, and it may hide the viscidia in one or two liquid-filled pouches. The fertile stigma part is located on the front side of the column. In Europe, only *Cypripedium* has a different column (see pp. 21–22).

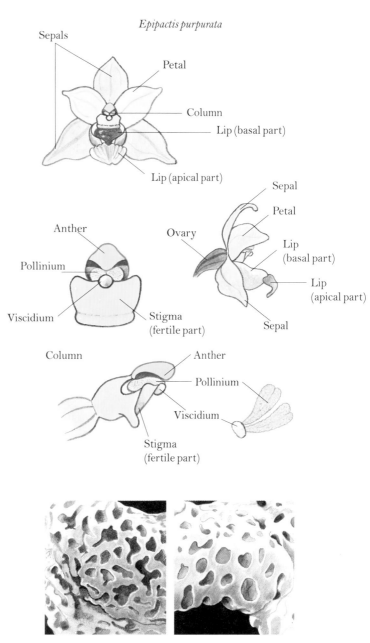

Surface structure of pollen ×2000. Left: *Epipactis palustris*; right: *E. purpurata*.

Classification of orchids

SCIENTIFIC CLASSIFICATION of plants has been attempted since the Middle Ages. Following the general acceptance of Darwin's seminal theories on evolution (i.e. since the late 1800s), there has been broad agreement that plants should be classified according to their most likely patterns of evolutionary relationship.

'Orchids' are defined as all plant species belonging to the orchid family (Orchidaceae). The orchid family is subdivided according to a hierarchical system that includes the main categories of (in decreasing order) subfamily, genus and species.

Among the five orchid subfamilies recognized worldwide, only three are represented in Europe. These are the Cypripedioideae (with one genus in Europe: *Cypripedium*), the Epidendroideae (with 10 genera in Europe: *Cephalanthera, Epipactis, Neottia, Limodorum, Epipogium, Hammarbya, Liparis, Malaxis, Calypso* and *Corallorhiza*) and the Orchidoideae to which the remaining 22 genera in Europe belong.

Scientific species names

In botanical classification, the fundamental category is the species. Any scientific name of a plant species consists of three elements, of which the two first are in Latin.

For instance, the Heath Spotted-orchid is called '*Dactylorhiza maculata* (L.) Soó'. The first element (*Dactylorhiza*) is the genus name, which is identical for all species belonging to the same genus. The second element (*maculata*) is called the specific epithet and indicates the species concerned. The same specific epithet may be used for species in different genera; it is the combination of genus name and specific epithet that makes a species name unique and unequivocal. The third element ((L.) Soó) consists of one or two author references – in this example Linnaeus (in parenthesis) who originally described the species as '*Orchis maculata* L.', followed by von Soó who later (due to his differing view on the systematic relationships of this species) published the currently accepted species name. In everyday use, it is common to abbreviate the genus name or to omit the author name(s), or both.

Subdivision of species

Highly variable species with two or more characteristic forms may be subdivided into subspecies (e.g. *Neotinea tridentata* ssp. *tridentata* versus ssp. *conica*) or into varieties (e.g. *Dactylorhiza incarnata* var. *incarnata* versus var. *ochroleuca*) – the variety being a hierarchically lower category than subspecies.

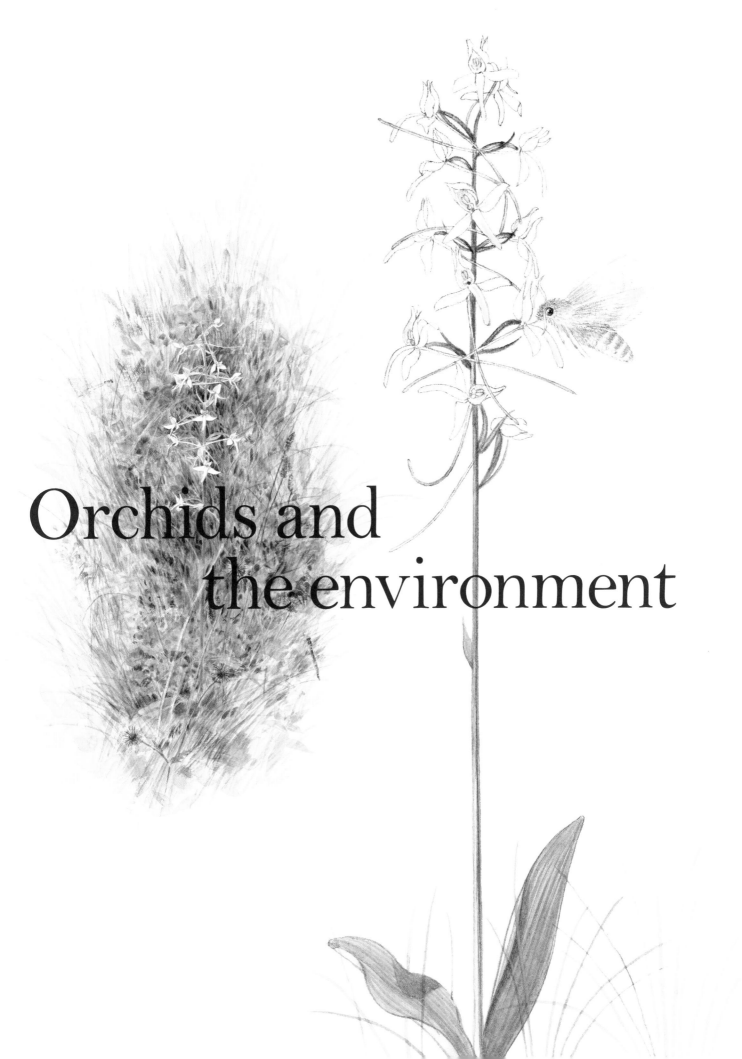

Orchids and
the environment

Orchids and fungi

I

N ALL EUROPEAN ORCHIDS, the fruit is a capsule that dries up and ruptures by longitudinal slits at maturity. Thousands of dust-like seeds from each capsule are then dispersed by the wind. Due to the tiny size of the seeds, their only reserves are microscopic bodies of fat and proteins inside the cells of the embryo – barely enough to nourish the very first stage of germination.

Germination

When an orchid seed germinates, the first organ to develop is a so-called protocorm, which is tiny and tuber-like. Soon, it develops into a more elongated 'mycorrhizome' that carries small scale-like leaves. The next steps are the formations of the root system and an aerial shoot. Usually, a number of years pass before a flowering shoot is produced.

In the laboratory, orchids can be raised from meristems (special tissue regions where cell divisions are responsible for the plant's growth) or germinated from seed in sterile nutrient media. In the wild, successful germination depends on the first formed structures becoming colonized by a suitable fungus that can be digested. This is the beginning of a long-term intimate connection known as mycorrhiza.

Mycorrhiza

One or more mycorrhizal fungi continuously inhabit the roots (if any) and often also the rhizome or tubers. The fungal hyphae usually enter through root hairs and colonize cells in the peripheral tissue. Here, they form dense coils (pelotons). At the inner boundary of the infected zone, the hyphae

Early growth from meristem
in sterile culture

Young shoot of *Cymbidium*
(tropical genus) ready
for removal of meristem

Orchid plantlets in test tube

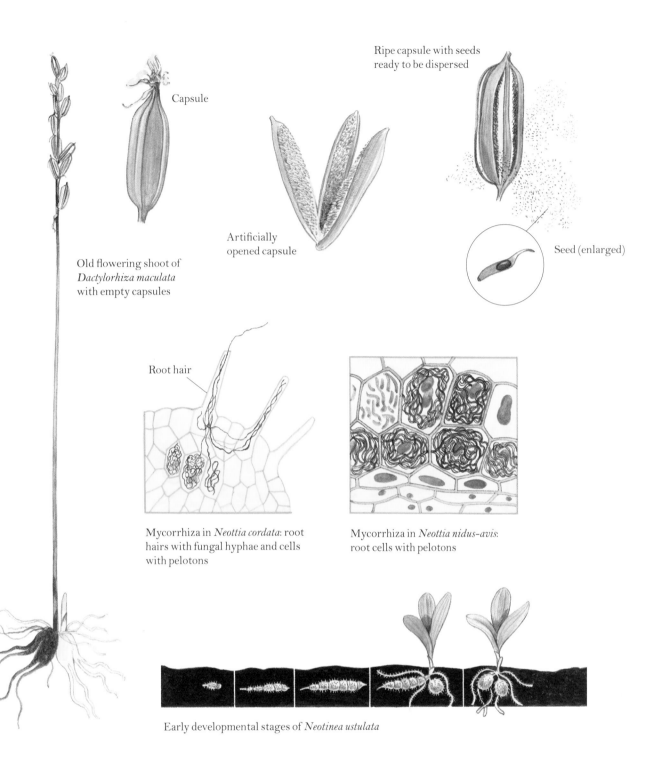

Capsule

Ripe capsule with seeds
ready to be dispersed

Artificially
opened capsule

Seed (enlarged)

Old flowering shoot of
Dactylorhiza maculata
with empty capsules

Root hair

Mycorrhiza in *Neottia cordata*: root
hairs with fungal hyphae and cells
with pelotons

Mycorrhiza in *Neottia nidus-avis*:
root cells with pelotons

Early developmental stages of *Neotinea ustulata*

are being digested. In this way, nutrients and chemical energy from the fungus are utilized by the orchid. In general, the orchid gives nothing in exchange (but see p. 68). Most orchids combine mycorrhizal nourishment with photosynthesis, but they can often survive several years completely underground thanks to their mycorrhiza. Species without green parts are fully dependent on mycorrhiza for life.

Pollination

POLLINATION IS THE PROCESS where pollen is deposited on a stigma in a flower. Following pollination, each pollen grain will produce a pollen tube that penetrates the stigma and grows through the style into the ovary. Here, individual pollen tubes will enter individual ovules and fertilize them. The fertilized ovules subsequently develop into seeds, and the ovary expands to form a fruit.

The pollen being deposited on a stigma may originate from the same flower (self-pollination in a narrow sense), from another flower in the same individual (self-pollination in a wider sense) or from a flower on a different individual (cross-pollination). Whereas pollination in most plants is effected by an external agent such as wind, water or animals, some species are capable of spontaneous self-pollination. Due to the lack of genetic recombination between individuals, self-pollination will gradually reduce genetic variation (and, hence, adaptability) of the species concerned. Therefore, high frequencies of cross-pollination usually represent an evolutionary advantage; but in rare cases, the consistently high seed set resulting from self-pollination amply counterbalances the disadvantages of this pollination mode.

Orchid pollination

In the vast majority of flowering plants, loose powdery pollen and a tendency towards modest fusion of the male and female organs in the flower seriously limit the degree to which pollination (especially cross-pollination) can be performed precisely and efficiently. In contrast, the fusion of male and female organs of the orchid flower into a column, the aggregation of pollen grains into much larger pollinia (in *Cypripedium* less well-defined pollen smears) and the ability to glue the pollinia to visiting insects must have been crucial preconditions for the evolution of the often highly specialized pollination mechanisms in orchids.

Selective advantages

Darwin was the first to suggest that the various pollination mechanisms found in orchids are the results of evolution through natural selection ('survival of the fittest'). Today, there is overwhelming evidence that Darwin was right. Selective advantages that in particular have favoured the evolution of specialized mechanisms, as well as other pollination-related specializations, appear to be: (1) reduced pollen loss, (2) increased frequency of cross-pollination relative to self-pollination and (3) reduced risk of hybridization. Incidentally, the probability of hybridization is not always limited through pollination-related specializations; more commonly, differences in distribution, local occurrence or flowering time constitute important barriers. Still, it is not exceptional to find natural orchid hybrids in Europe.

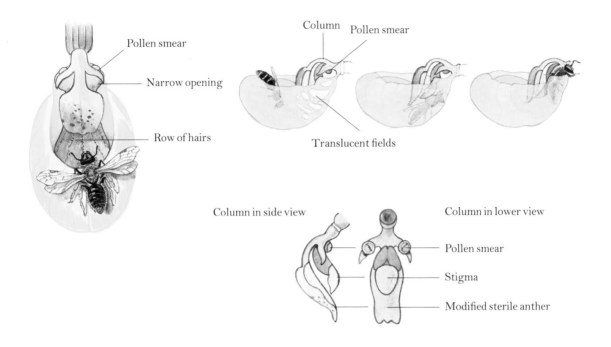

Attraction, rewards and deception

Insect-pollinated orchids attract pollinators by floral scent and by their visual display of flowers; the relative importance and roles of these attractants vary. Once arrived on a flower, the insect will search for a reward such as pollen, nectar or shelter. Whereas no European orchid offers pollen for consumption, *Serapias* flowers provide shelter, and nectar production is systematically widespread. In some species the nectar is freely accessible to any visiting insect; in others it is hidden in a spur where it can only be reached by specific insects with precisely fitting mouthparts. Partly because of this, the diversity of pollinators varies considerably among orchid species.

Many European orchid species produce no reward, but are pollinated through deceit.

This may occur via 'generalized food deception' (attraction through a general similarity to rewarding plant species), 'Batesian floral mimicry' (attraction through precise imitation of the flowers of a particular rewarding species) or 'sexual deception' (attraction through imitation of female insect mating signals).

A number of European orchids are spontaneously self-pollinating, either consistently or as a back-up solution in the absence of pollinator visits. However, since high frequencies of cross-pollination generally represent an evolutionary advantage, it is hardly surprising that most species are adapted to insect pollination. A few examples of adaptations are outlined below.

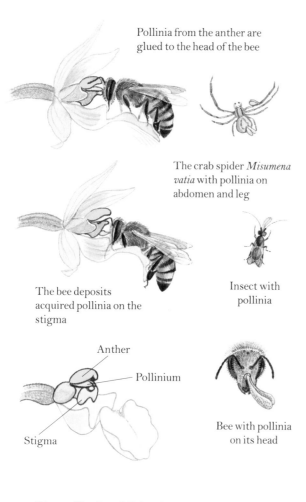

The Western Honey Bee (*Apis mellifera*) pollinates *Epipactis palustris*

Pollinia from the anther are glued to the head of the bee

The crab spider *Misumena vatia* with pollinia on abdomen and leg

The bee deposits acquired pollinia on the stigma

Insect with pollinia

Anther

Pollinium

Stigma

Bee with pollinia on its head

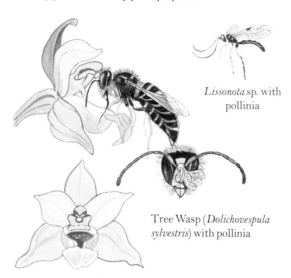

Wasp pollination of *Epipactis purpurata*

Lissonota sp. with pollinia

Tree Wasp (*Dolichovespula sylvestris*) with pollinia

Example 1
One-way traffic promotes outcrossing

Cypripedium is the only European orchid genus that has a flower structure that in several different ways differs from the common scheme described on pp. 14–15. Thus, the *Cypripedium* flower has two fertile anthers (rather than one), and they are placed on short lateral branches that represent strongly reduced filaments. Furthermore, the pollen grains form a paste-like pollen smear (rather than solid pollinia), and the sterile median anther forms a strongly modified, shield-like structure.

Cypripedium calceolus is pollinated by certain solitary bees. A visiting bee will enter the slipper-shaped lip, but as this contains no reward, the bee attempts to leave soon after its entry. However, due to the incurved slippery walls, the bee cannot leave through the main opening. Its only option is to crawl along the hairy back-wall until it reaches the junction between lip and column. Here it can force its way out at either side; but in doing so it presses its back against the stigma (depositing previously acquired pollen, if any) and then one of the two anthers (acquiring a new pollen smear). The fixed sequence of contact with stigma and anther increases the probability of cross-pollination.

Example 2
Different degrees of outcrossing in one genus

Epipactis palustris (mainly bee-pollinated) and *E. purpurata* (wasp-pollinated) secrete nectar in the basal, concave part of the lip. The pollinia are glued to the pollinator by a diffuse viscidium produced from the sterile tip of the stigma. Whereas *E. palustris* shows a high rate of outcrossing (partly due to its

Pollination of *Neottia ovata*

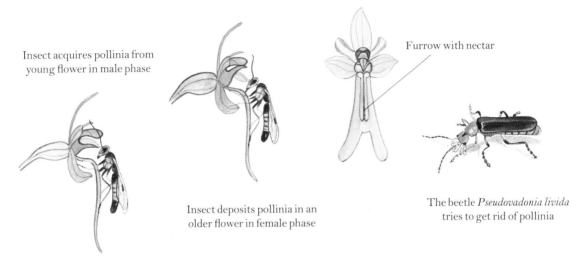

Insect acquires pollinia from young flower in male phase

Insect deposits pollinia in an older flower in female phase

Furrow with nectar

The beetle *Pseudovadonia livida* tries to get rid of pollinia

Moth pollination of *Platanthera chlorantha*

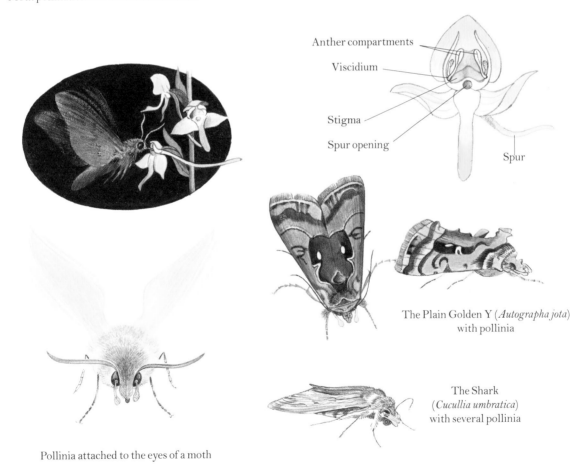

Anther compartments

Viscidium

Stigma

Spur opening

Spur

Pollinia attached to the eyes of a moth

The Plain Golden Y (*Autographa jota*) with pollinia

The Shark (*Cucullia umbratica*) with several pollinia

Pollination of *Anacamptis pyramidalis*

The Small Elephant Hawk-moth (*Deilephila porcellus*) probes a spur in search of nectar

Anther

Stigma lobes

Spur opening

Position of pollinia on proboscis just after being removed from the flower

Position of pollinia a little while later

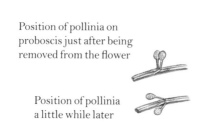

The Small Elephant Hawk-moth with pollinia on its proboscis

Heath Fritillary (*Melitaea athalia*)

widely separated flowers), *E. purpurata* has a high rate of pollen transfer within the same inflorescence, because the wasps tend to crawl from flower to flower in the dense racemes.

Example 3
Temporal change of sex function in flowers

Neottia ovata has an adaptation that effectively prevents self-pollination. In a newly opened flower, the fertile part of the stigma is blocked by the down-curved median stigma lobe, which is sterile. However, when the pollinia are removed by an insect, the median stigma lobe will start turning upwards, exposing the fertile stigma part. Thus, in a few hours the flower changes from a functioning male to female.

Example 4
Small differences in flower morphology largely prevent hybridization

Platanthera chlorantha is pollinated by moths feeding on nectar that is concealed in a long spur. The spur is usually longer than the proboscis of the moth, so to reach as deep down as possible, the moth presses its head against the column. As the anther compartments are widely separated, the two pollinia with individual viscidia will be glued to the eyes of the moth, and in this position they will fit perfectly into the broad stigma of another *P. chlorantha* flower. The column structure largely prevents hybridization with the likewise moth-pollinated *P. bifolia* (see pp. 85–86). In the latter, the anther compartments are close together (implying that the pollinia will be glued to the proboscis of the moth), and the stigma is very narrow.

Example 5
Delayed pollinium movements promote outcrossing

Anacamptis pyramidalis likewise has a long spur, but it contains no nectar. The proboscis of a visiting butterfly or moth will touch a viscidium, which then glues the pollinia to the proboscis. At first, the pollinia are erect and therefore will not hit the fertile stigma lobes on either side of the anther base. However, the pollinia gradually diverge and eventually reach a horizontal position suitable for pollination; but the delay means that the insect has probably moved to another inflorescence in the meantime. Found in several genera, delayed movements of pollinia are a common adaptation that increases the frequency of cross-pollination.

Example 6
Pollination through sexual deception

Ophrys insectifera ssp. *insectifera* is pollinated through sexual deceit of the males of two species of digger wasps. The floral scent precisely imitates the female sex pheromone and attracts the males at considerable distance. A visual similarity between the dark flower parts and the female wasp undoubtedly plays a role for short-distance attraction and, especially, for making the male assume a longitudinal position on the lip. Details of the lip hairiness induce the male to orientate its head towards the column. Probably as a response to combined stimuli from scent and hairiness, the male now attempts mating with the lip! During this process, known as pseudocopulation, the wasp repeatedly presses his head against the column, leading to deposition or acquisition of pollinia, or both. Pollination through pseudocopulation strongly prevails in *Ophrys*, and it seems to have a high degree of species-specificity.

The digger wasp *Argogorytes mystaceus* pollinates *Ophrys insectifera* ssp. *insectifera*

Female

A male attempts mating with the lip of the flower

Pollinia glued to the head of a male wasp

Where to find orchids

THE EUROPEAN LANDSCAPE ranges from around sea level to 4,810 m elevation and has soils of virtually any possible texture, moisture, acidity and nutrient content. The climate is subtropical to temperate (with a few Norwegian islands being truly Arctic), and the annual extremes and range of both precipitation and temperature vary widely across the continent. This setting supports complex patterns of communities of plants, animals, fungi and other biological organisms.

Whether or not a local site can accommodate one or more orchid populations depends on whether the habitat (i.e. the combined environmental profile of the site) fulfils all the ecological requirements of the orchids concerned. Most orchid species exhibit various degrees of specialization pertaining to the growth requirements of adult plants and to transient life events such as germination and pollination. Some requirements are concerned with the physical and chemical environment, others with the organismal community (including, for example, mycorrhiza-forming fungi and pollinating insects).

Orchids are poor competitors

If cultivated in isolation, most orchids are fairly tolerant to variation in the physical and chemical environment. However, they are poor competitors, so the range of conditions under which an orchid species can cope in the wild is often narrow and involves soil with only a moderate nutrient content. Most orchids are found: (1) in habitats with recently exposed soil (the vegetation still being dominated by pioneer species), (2) in mature natural habitats with limited competition (e.g. due to low light levels) or (3) in semi-natural habitats where human utilization affects the balance of competition among species.

Orchid habitats

Particularly important orchid habitats in northern and central Europe include dune slacks, fens, marshes, hay meadows, grassland, alpine meadows and heaths, wooded meadows, recently abandoned chalk/marl pits and forests of long temporal continuity. In all of these habitats, basic soils tend to support more orchids. Few orchid species occur in bogs, lowland heaths or other habitats characterized by soils of considerable acidity.

The lowlands of southern Europe are dominated by subtropical habitats not encountered north of the Mediterranean region. Open pine forests and low, semi-natural scrubs (usually referred to as garrigue or phrygana) can be especially rich in orchids. The Azores, Madeira and the Canary Islands, all under the influence of the Gulf Stream and northern trade winds, offer laurel forests and scrubs as additional orchid habitats.

Calcareous meadow with Gymnadenia conopsea, *Öland, Sweden*

Threats and conservation

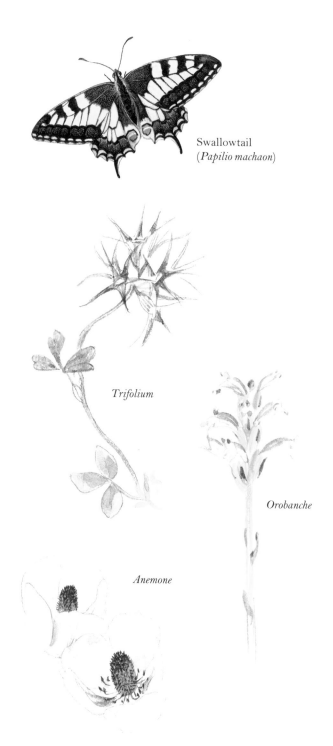

M OST EUROPEAN ORCHID species have declined in frequency (and often in distribution) over the past decades, mainly due to changes in land use and agricultural practices. Consequently, many species are now included in national and regional 'red lists' of extinct, endangered and vulnerable species. Depending on the kind of threat, the decline can be counteracted by different conservation measures.

Indirect threats

Reclaiming of land for mining, construction work or cultivation of annual crops has destroyed thousands of European orchid habitats since the beginning of the industrial revolution. In later years, nature reserves have been set up, habitats have been established or re-established, and exhausted pits and fields have been left for natural re-colonization – but only on a minor scale.

Orchids in mature natural habitats (usually old forests) are highly sensitive to environmental disturbance, whereas orchids in semi-natural habitats (such as hay meadows, grassland and garrigue) rely on the intensity of utilization being within the narrow range that enables them to compete with associated species. Thus, appropriate habitat management, including measures against invasive species, is crucial for long-term conservation of orchid populations.

Swallowtail (*Papilio machaon*)

Trifolium

Orobanche

Anemone

Aegilops

Orchid habitats, like this near Agios Nikolaos in Crete, are also important to organisms other than orchids. Conservation of orchid habitats assists the survival of a multitude of plant and animal species

Direct threats

Traditionally, orchids have been among the favourite objects of plant collectors. In Europe, collection of tubers for consumption is restricted to the south-eastern border districts. Other purposes are widespread, but have changed over time.

Scientific collection used to be common, but rarely targeted more than a few individuals in each population. Besides, it now has become largely replaced by photography and less destructive sampling. Collection for ornamental purposes increased as scientific collection decreased, and sometimes entire populations have been ripped out. In most of Europe, some or all orchid species are now protected by law, and a few re-introduction programmes have been conducted.

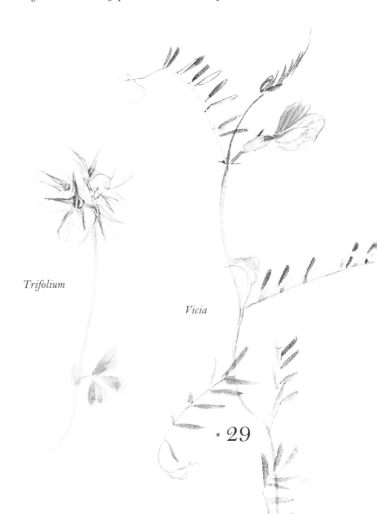

Trifolium

Vicia

* 29

Distribution

ORCHIDS CAN BE FOUND almost throughout Europe, from around sea level to *c*.2,900 m elevation. However, the upper altitudinal limit of orchid occurrence decreases with increasing latitude, and no orchids occur on the Arctic islands of northern Norway. Species richness generally increases with decreasing latitude, reaching its European maxima in Italy and Greece. Individual species ranges within Europe can be coherent or slightly to strongly fragmented.

Three European species have aberrant total distributions: *Gennaria diphylla* (western Mediterranean, Canary Islands, Madeira), *Platanthera hyperborea* (Greenland, Iceland) and *Ophrys atlantica* (Mediterranean North Africa, southern Spain). All remaining orchid species occurring in Europe can be roughly classified into three overall distribution types that are characterized below. Subspecies and varieties are often more narrowly distributed.

Species on both sides of the Atlantic

Seven species (e.g. *Neottia cordata, Hammarbya paludosa*) have a nearly continuous distribution in the land areas of the northern hemisphere. In addition, *Liparis loeselii, Spiranthes romanzoffiana* and *Pseudorchis albida* also occur on both sides of the Atlantic, but their individual distributions are much smaller on one or both sides of the ocean. Finally, a few European species have been artificially introduced to North America, but such occurrences are ignored in this survey.

Species in Europe and Asia

About 85 of the European orchid species have a total range that combines their (small to large) European distribution with occurrence in various parts of temperate to subtropical Asia, and in some cases in Mediterranean parts of North Africa.

Species restricted to Europe

Around 35 species are restricted to Europe. Here, most of them are more or less widely distributed (e.g. *Epipactis leptochila, Dactylorhiza sambucina, Ophrys insectifera, Chamorchis alpina*). A smaller number are 'endemic', meaning that their total distribution is very small (for example just encompassing a single island, a single archipelago or one small mountain range). Endemic species depicted in this book include, for example: *Cephalanthera cucullata* (Crete), *Goodyera macrophylla* (Madeira), *Habenaria tridactylites* (Canary Islands), *Gymnigritella runei* (northern Sweden) and *Orchis sitiaca* (Crete).

Orchid
portraits

Cypripedium

* SLIPPER ORCHIDS *

Long-lived orchids with kettle traps

THE EUROPEAN SPECIES mainly occur in partial shade in meadows, scrub and open woodland, although *C. calceolus* and *C. macranthos* may occasionally grow fully exposed. Whereas *C. calceolus* is restricted to basic soils and *C. guttatum* requires neutral to weakly acid soils, *C. macranthos* can cope with this whole range of acidity. The flowering time is spring to summer.

Cypripedium differs from all other European orchids in having two fertile anthers that produce pollen smears rather than solid pollinia and in the column being dominated by a large, shield-like structure formed by a sterile anther. More eye-catching features include the large size of the flowers, the slipper-like lip and largely fused lateral sepals.

On the global scale, around 47 species of *Cypripedium* are known, but only three of them occur in Europe. The total distribution is limited to the northern hemisphere, mainly encompassing temperate regions. The range extends from Europe across Siberia to eastern Asia (where representatives can be found from the Himalayas to Kamchatka) and also covers most of North and Central America.

Longevity

The horizontal, usually branched rhizome is strongly condensed and therefore produces a dense aggregation of leafy and flowering shoots. Such a coherent group of individual shoots is referred to as a clone. The clones of some *Cypripedium* species can grow very old; ages up to 192 years have been estimated for *C. calceolus* in Estonia.

Pollination

Cypripedium belongs to the group of so-called slipper orchids, being so named because of their slipper- to pitcher-shaped lip. This constitutes a 'kettle trap' that prevents any visiting insect from leaving the lip through its main opening. Instead, the potential pollinator is kept prisoner until it discovers one of two troublesome escape routes at the rear end of the lip. Following either route, the insect will have to press its back against the stigma and one of the anthers on its way out, and in doing so it first pollinates the flower with foreign pollen (if any) and subsequently acquires a new pollen smear. For a detailed account on pollination in *C. calceolus*, see page 22. *Cypripedium guttatum* is pollinated by sweat bees (Halictidae), *C. calceolus* by sweat bees and various species of mining bee (*Andrena*). *Cypripedium macranthos* appears to be pollinated exclusively by bumblebee queens.

Öland, Sweden

Cypripedium calceolus

LADY'S-SLIPPER

15–60(–70) cm; spring to early summer; from temperate and subarctic parts of Europe
(west to England and the Pyrenees) across Siberia to Manchuria and Sakhalin.

Uppland, Sweden

Cypripedium calceolus
LADY'S-SLIPPER
data given on page 33.

Visiting fly

1

From herbarium specimen

2

From cultivated plant

Cypripedium guttatum

SPOTTED LADY'S-SLIPPER

(1) 15–35 cm; late spring to summer; from European
Russia to China, Korea and Kamchatka – and from
Alaska to Yukon.

Cypripedium macranthos

LARGE-FLOWERED LADY'S-SLIPPER

(2) 15–50 cm; summer; from Belarus across Siberia to
temperate eastern Asia.

Cephalanthera

* HELLEBORINES *

Floral mimicry and more

MOST MEMBERS OF this genus are true forest plants. However, some species (especially *C. damasonium* and *C. longifolia*) also occur in scrub and wooded meadows. More or less basic soils are generally required, except by the more broadly tolerant *C. longifolia*. The flowering time is spring to summer.

Cephalanthera is primarily characterized by the combination of: (1) a stem with alternating green leaves and (2) the lip being divided into a concave to short-spurred basal part and a flat to channelled apical part that bears 3-6 longitudinal ridges. The white or purple versatile anther and the sessile ovary are also noteworthy.

The genus contains about 15 species and has a total range that includes three main areas: (1) most of Europe together with adjoining Mediterranean parts of North Africa, Asia Minor and the Middle East; (2) an area in mainland South-East Asia, from the Himalayas and Myanmar to Japan and Manchuria; (3) the western part of the USA.

Pollination

Most observations of pollination in *C. rubra* have indicated that this orchid is usually pollinated by bees of the genus *Chelostoma* (family Megachilidae). The females of these bees collect pollen almost exclusively from species of bellflower (*Campanula*), and also the much more mobile males are strongly associated with bellflowers. In Gotland it has been demonstrated that *Cephalanthera rubra* attracts the *Chelostoma* bees by mimicking (imitating) the flower colour of bellflowers. To the human eye, the colour of the orchid flower is distinctly different, but in the range of bee vision, the mimic and the model have nearly identical reflectance. Furthermore, the crested ridges on the orchid labellum may mimic the sexual organs of bellflowers. *Cephalanthera rubra* is usually pollinated by *Chelostoma* males that mistake the *Cephalanthera* flowers for *Campanula* during mate-seeking flights; the relative number of fruits set in the orchid is several times smaller at sites that are virtually unpatrolled by the bellflower-associated species of *Chelostoma*.

Cephalanthera longifolia has been claimed to mimic the flowers of Sage-leaved Cistus (*Cistus salviifolius*); but documentation is poor, and the orchid is much more widely distributed than the alleged model. In *C. damasonium*, self-pollination occurs spontaneously while the flower is still in bud. Pollination has not yet been studied in the remaining European species.

Gotland, Sweden

Cephalanthera rubra

RED HELLEBORINE

10–65(–75) cm; summer; most of the Mediterranean region,
the Caucasus and temperate Europe north to southern Norway.

Crete, Greece

Acorn cup of *Quercus coccifera*
from the same site

Cephalanthera cucullata

HOODED HELLEBORINE

10–30 cm; late spring to early summer; Crete.

Alexandropolis, Greece

The Crimea

Cephalanthera epipactoides

SPURRED HELLEBORINE

(1) 15–70(–100) cm; spring to early summer; eastern
Greece, northern and western Turkey.

Cephalanthera longifolia

NARROW–LEAVED HELLEBORINE

(2) (10–)20–70 cm; spring to early summer; temperate
Europe (excluding the northernmost and north-
easternmost parts), most of the Mediterranean region and
extending further east to the Himalayas.

Öland, Sweden

Cephalanthera longifolia

NARROW–LEAVED HELLEBORINE

data given on page 39.

Mon, Denmark

Gotland, Sweden

Cephalanthera damasonium

WHITE HELLEBORINE

15–60 cm; late spring to early summer; from England across central and southern Europe,
Anatolia, the Crimea and the Caucasus to Iran – and with apparently isolated occurrences in
China and the eastern Himalayas.

Epipactis

✳ HELLEBORINES ✳

Spanning the range from cross- to self-pollination

Most *EPIPACTIS* SPECIES are forest plants, although several may also occur in scrub or even on grassland or dunes. The only exception in Europe is *E. palustris*, which mainly grows in calcareous fens and marshes, but also on chalk grassland. Most species are summer-flowering, with *E. microphylla* and *E. purpurata* locally being earlier or later, respectively.

Epipactis is primarily characterized by the lip being divided into a concave to bowl-shaped basal part and a flat apical part with irregular thickenings. However, the combination of alternating leaves and spreading to pendulous flowers with a versatile yellow anther and a shortly to distinctly stalked ovary is also noteworthy.

Species delimitation is problematic; 15–70 species may be recognized worldwide, and most of them occur in Europe. The natural distribution extends from Europe across temperate Asia to Japan, and from southernmost Arabia to tropical Africa, with one additional species (*E. gigantea*) in western North America. Additionally, *E. helleborine* has been introduced to North America where it is now widespread.

Mycorrhiza

Mycorrhizal partners are mainly sac fungi that also form mycorrhiza with trees. Due to well-developed mycorrhiza, individual *Epipactis* plants can live completely underground for long periods (underground survival for up to 18 years has been documented). White to violet individuals incapable of photosynthesis are occasionally encountered. They are fully dependent on their fungus as a carbon source.

Pollination

Most European species are mainly pollinated by bees or wasps foraging on nectar in the basal part of the lip. In these species, the sterile tip of the stigma forms a barrier between the anther and the receptive stigma part, and it produces a drop of membrane-covered adhesive. When a visiting insect touches this structure, the membrane ruptures, and the adhesive attaches the fragile pollinia to the insect. The insect may subsequently deposit the pollinia, or fragments of them, on the stigma of the same or other *Epipactis* flowers. Some species appear to be adapted for insect-mediated pollen transfer within the same inflorescence, and in other species the flowers are capable of unassisted self-pollination. The latter phenomenon seems to have evolved recurrently through reduction of the barrier between the anther and the receptive stigma part.

Öland, Sweden

Epipactis palustris

MARSH HELLEBORINE

7–70(–90) cm; summer; Europe (excluding the northernmost and southernmost parts)
and across temperate Asia to Mongolia.

Öland, Sweden

Epipactis atrorubens ssp. *atrorubens*

DARK-RED HELLEBORINE

(10–)20–80(–100) cm; summer; from Europe (excluding Iceland, the Iberian Peninsula
and major Mediterranean islands) across Siberia to Tomsk.

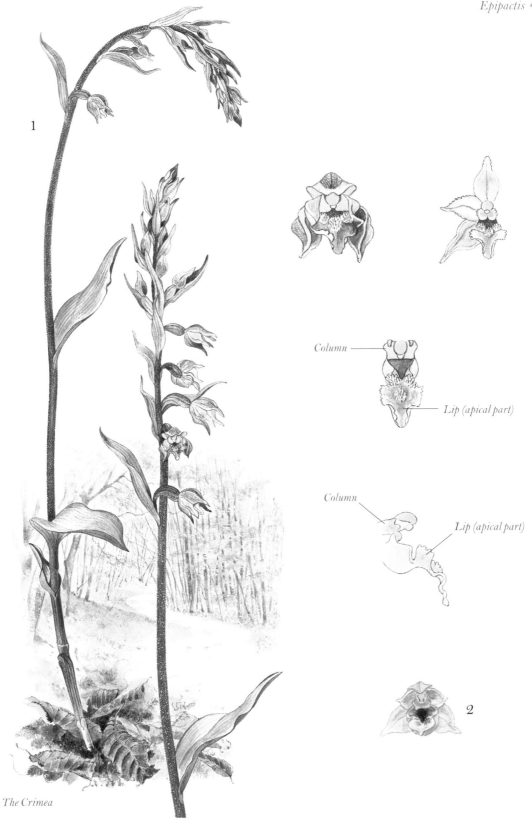

The Crimea

Column

Lip (apical part)

Column

Lip (apical part)

Epipactis microphylla

SMALL-LEAVED HELLEBORINE

(1) 15–55 cm; late spring to late summer; from central and
southern Europe across Anatolia to the Caucasus and Iran.

Epipactis provincialis

PROVENCE HELLEBORINE

(2) 17–50 cm; early summer; southern France.

Öland, Sweden

1

2

Epipactis helleborine

BROAD-LEAVED HELLEBORINE

(1) ssp. *helleborine*; 18–90(–130) cm; late summer; from Mediterranean North Africa
and most of Europe to Siberia, the Himalayas and China – and widespread as a naturalized alien in North America.
(2) ssp. *neerlandica*; 10–50(–90) cm; late summer; Wales and along the Channel and North Sea coasts
of mainland Europe from France to southern Norway.

Jutland, Denmark

Epipactis purpurata

VIOLET HELLEBORINE

(10–)15–80(–120) cm; late summer to early autumn; from England, France and north-eastern Spain across central
Europe to Denmark in the north, Lithuania in the north-east and Greece, Romania, Moldavia and possibly the
Ukraine in the south-east.

Öland, Sweden

Epipactis phyllanthes

GREEN-FLOWERED HELLEBORINE

8–55(–70) cm; summer; scattered in western Europe (between northern Spain,
Northern Ireland and southern Sweden).

Germany

Møn, Denmark

Epipactis muelleri ssp. *muelleri*

MÜLLER'S HELLEBORINE

(1) 20–90 cm; summer; scattered in central and
southern Europe.

Epipactis leptochila ssp. *leptochila*

NARROW-LIPPED HELLEBORINE

(2) 16–80 cm; late summer; from England and
Denmark across central Europe to the Pyrenees
and the Balkan Peninsula.

Neottia

* BIRD'S-NEST ORCHID & TWAYBLADES *
Sex change of individual flowers

NEOTTIA CORDATA is a plant of poor, usually mossy ground in conifer forest, moist willow scrubs, subalpine heaths and birch woods. In contrast, the other European species require nutrient-rich soils; *N. nidus-avis* grows in woodland, whereas *N. ovata* occurs in a broad range of habitats, including forest, coppices, meadows, grassland and dune slacks. The flowering time is late spring to summer.

Neottia is primarily characterized by having distinctly stalked flowers with an unspurred and hairless lip that is cleft for at least one-third of its length. Two of the European species have two green leaves placed opposite each other on the lower part of the stem, whereas the third species has a few brown, strongly reduced leaves alternating on the stem.

On the global scale, around 60 species of *Neottia* are known, but only three occur in Europe. The total distribution covers major parts of the temperate (to subtropical) zone of the northern hemisphere, mainly excepting large areas in central Asia. As delimited here, *Neottia* also covers the previously recognized genus *Listera*.

Change of functional sex

Column function in *Neottia* is remarkable (see also p. 24). The anther ruptures before the flower opens, leaving the two pollinia resting upon the flap-like sterile part of the stigma. The margins of the flap are curled around the pollinia and position them with their narrow end just below its tip. When the tip of the flap is touched by an insect, a droplet of adhesive, kept under pressure in a series of enlarged cells, is shot onto the visitor, and the margins of the flap reflex so that the protruding pollinia are glued to the insect. Consequently, the pollinia are extracted when the insect backs away from the column. The sterile flap initially blocks the fertile stigma part, but in *c.*2–24 hours upon extraction of the pollinia (duration mainly depending on the species) the sterile flap lifts and exposes the fertile stigma part.

Thus, the flowers of *Neottia* generally pass a male phase before entering a female phase. However, in *N. nidus-avis*, the above mechanism is poorly developed and promotes rather than prevents spontaneous self-pollination. *Neottia cordata* is mainly pollinated by fungus gnats, whereas *N. ovata* has a diverse pollinator fauna that is often dominated by sawflies and parasitic wasps. All *Neottia* species offer nectar as a reward.

Uppland, Sweden

Neottia cordata

LESSER TWAYBLADE

4–20(–25) cm; late spring to summer; northern to central Europe,
northern to central Asia and subarctic to temperate North America.

*Parasitic wasp
bearing pollinia*

Öland, Sweden

Neottia ovata

COMMON TWAYBLADE

(13–)25–75 cm; late spring to summer; from most of Europe across temperate Asia to Altai and the Himalayas –
and as an introduced alien in Ontario, Canada.

Monte Gargano, Italy

Remains of fruiting plant
from the preceding year

Neottia nidus-avis

BIRD'S-NEST ORCHID

8–35(–50) cm; late spring to summer; from most of Europe across Siberia to Sakhalin,
and across the Crimea and northern Anatolia to Iran and the Caucasus.

Limodorum

* LIMODORES *
Dynamic dependency on fungi and pollinators

P LANTS BELONGING TO this genus are usually found in oak forest, pine woods, abandoned wine fields and Mediterranean scrub where they grow in basic or neutral (to weakly acid) soil. The flowering time is spring to summer.

Limodorum is easily recognized by the combination of: (1) a stout stem only provided with scale leaves, (2) large purplish flowers (lateral sepals more than 15 mm long) and (3) erect ovaries.

The total distribution encompasses the Caucasus, the Mediterranean region and neighbouring warm-temperate parts of western and central Europe. Besides the widely distributed *L. abortivum*, the genus only contains the western to central Mediterranean *L. trabutianum* (not illustrated in this book; characterized by its narrow, petal-like lip with only a rudimentary spur).

Mycorrhiza

Limodorum forms mycorrhiza with various fungi, mainly the Milk White Brittlegill (*Russula delica*) and some of its close relatives. The same fungi form a different kind of mycorrhiza with certain woody plants, so the latter may serve as an important ultimate carbon source for the orchid. However, it should be noted that *Limodorum* plants can also photosynthesize to a limited extent, and that the photosynthetic contribution may be increased to compensate for low levels of fungal carbon delivery and to support seed development.

Pollination

In *L. trabutianum* the stigma is perpendicular to the axis of the anther, so when the anther ruptures, the pollinia fall directly onto the fertile stigma part. Self-pollination usually happens while the plant is still in the bud stage; indeed, most flowers open just very slightly or not at all, but they always set fruit successfully. Thus, *L. trabutianum* is consistently self-pollinating.

In *L. abortivum* the stigma is parallel to the axis of the anther, for which reason self-pollination does not occur as quickly and easily as in *L. trabutianum*. Nevertheless, most populations of *L. abortivum* do reproduce entirely through self-pollination. In spite of the viscidium being placed on the upper stigmatic margin, the pollinia can touch the fertile stigma part at either side of the viscidium; from there, pollen tubes start growing and attach the pollinia firmly to the stigma. However, in a minority of populations, bees (mainly species of *Anthophora*) play a certain role as pollinators when visiting the flowers to forage on nectar offered in the spur.

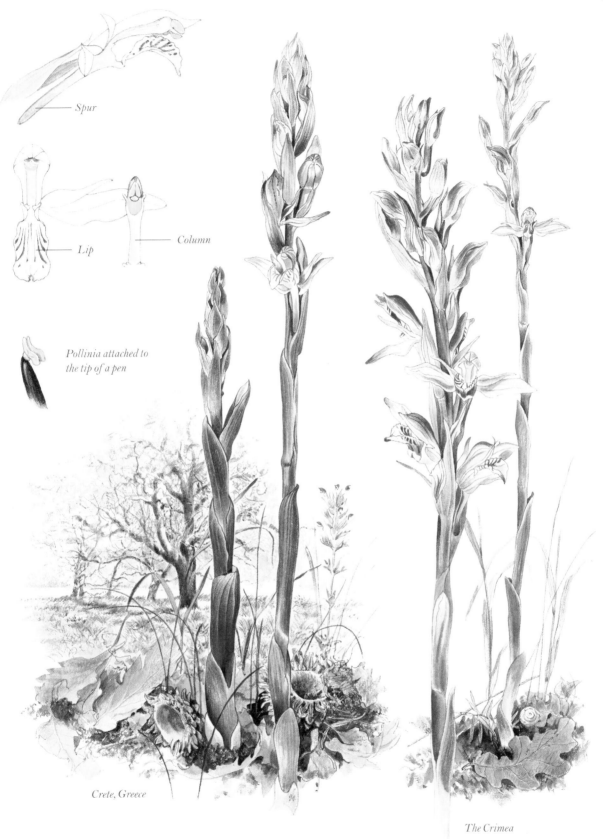

Spur

Lip

Column

*Pollinia attached to
the tip of a pen*

Crete, Greece

The Crimea

Limodorum abortivum

VIOLET BIRD'S-NEST ORCHID

20–80 cm; spring to summer; the Caucasus,
the Mediterranean region and adjoining warm-temperate parts of Europe.

Epipogium

* GHOST ORCHIDS *
Evasive 'ghosts' of the dark forest

E PIPOGIUM APHYLLUM, the only European species of this genus, is restricted to dark forest environments with high humidity. Most populations are found on humus-rich, calcareous ground under beech, spruce or fir. Flowering normally occurs in late summer, although solitary blooming individuals may occasionally be found as early as June or as late as October.

Epipogium is easily recognized by the combination of: (1) a fragile stem only provided with scale leaves, (2) pendent flowers with the labellum placed on the upper side (due to neither the ovary nor its stalk being twisted) and (3) the lip bearing 4–6 long warty ridges and forming a 6–8 mm long spur at the base.

This genus of just 3–4 species is distributed in tropical Africa and from Europe across Siberia to Kamchatka and Japan. From there, it extends further south through East and South-East Asia to Malesia, north-eastern Australia and the south-western Pacific islands.

Mycorrhiza and flowering

Having no roots and lacking photosynthetic abilities, *Epipogium* plants depend completely on digestion of various mycorrhizal fungi that colonize the short rhizome. The same genera of fungi are known to form mycorrhiza with various forest trees, so it seems likely that the orchids are ultimately nourished by surrounding trees.

Epipogium aphyllum has a reputation of highly erratic flowering – hence one of its vernacular names: Ghost Orchid. There has been much speculation as to which weather conditions may facilitate flowering, but hardly any statistical support has been presented. Adding to the secretive nature of the species, rare cases of underground flowering have been reported.

Propagation

Newly opened flowers of *E. aphyllum* emit a sweet, somewhat banana-like scent, but they do not produce nectar. bumblebee workers act as pollinators, but at most sites pollination rarely occurs. By the time the open flower is 3–4 days old, the anther has already turned from versatile to firmly attached, after which point the pollinia can no longer be extracted.

In *E. aphyllum*, vegetative propagation can happen in two ways. First, tips of rhizome branches may become detached and develop into separate plants. Secondly, underground runners are produced from the rhizome and produce tiny bulbils placed at 2.5–6 cm intervals; when the runners decay during autumn, the bulbils are detached and may develop into new individuals.

Jämtland, Sweden

Epipogium aphyllum

GHOST ORCHID

(5–)10–30 cm; late summer; from Europe (excluding Iceland, Ireland, Scotland and
the Mediterranean lowland) across temperate Asia to Japan and Kamchatka.

Hammarbya

* BOG ORCHID *

False epiphytes with cucumber-scented flowers

THIS TINY ORCHID is restricted to acid, nutrient-poor conditions in bogs, fens and wet dune slacks. In bogs, it usually grows on top of a layer of Bog Moss (*Sphagnum*) which is so thick that the orchid has no direct contact with the soil below. Because of this, *Hammarbya* is occasionally claimed to be an epiphyte; but, as the orchid is not physically attached to the 'host plant', *Hammarbya* is not an epiphyte in the traditional sense. Flowering occurs in late summer.

Hammarbya is mainly characterized by the combination of: (1) bracts that are at least half as long as the stalked ovaries, (2) weakly cucumber-scented tiny flowers with the lip placed on the upper side (due to the ovary being twisted 360°), (3) recurved petals that are shorter than the sepals and (4) a straight, ovate, acute lip that lacks a spur and is pale green with four darker longitudinal bands. It is also worth noting that the leaves are mostly three in number and usually shorter than 2.5 cm; they often produce marginal bulbils at the tip (see note on vegetative reproduction, p. 13).

The genus only consists of one species, which is distributed in major parts of the northern hemisphere. From Norway and the British Isles it extends across northern, central and eastern Europe, and onwards through Siberia to Sakhalin, Japan and Kamchatka. On the American side of the Pacific Ocean, *Hammarbya* ranges from Alaska through Canada to Ontario.

Environmental effects

The rhizome length varies markedly among individuals. This phenomenon is closely linked to the local environment. Where *Hammarbya* grows on more or less bare ground, for example in dune slacks, the rhizome is very short. In contrast, when the orchid grows among bog mosses, the yearly increment of the rhizome is several centimetres – a necessary precaution for the plant to keep up with the growth of the living substrate.

Populations of *H. paludosa* often fluctuate dramatically in size. The species is highly sensitive to changes in the water level and moisture of the substrate, and periods of draught may cause significant reductions in population size from one year to another.

Pollination

The cucumber-like scent emitted by the flowers is more distinct in newly opened blooms. The scent attracts small insects, especially mosquitoes and gnats, which serve as efficient pollinators when foraging on the sparse nectar.

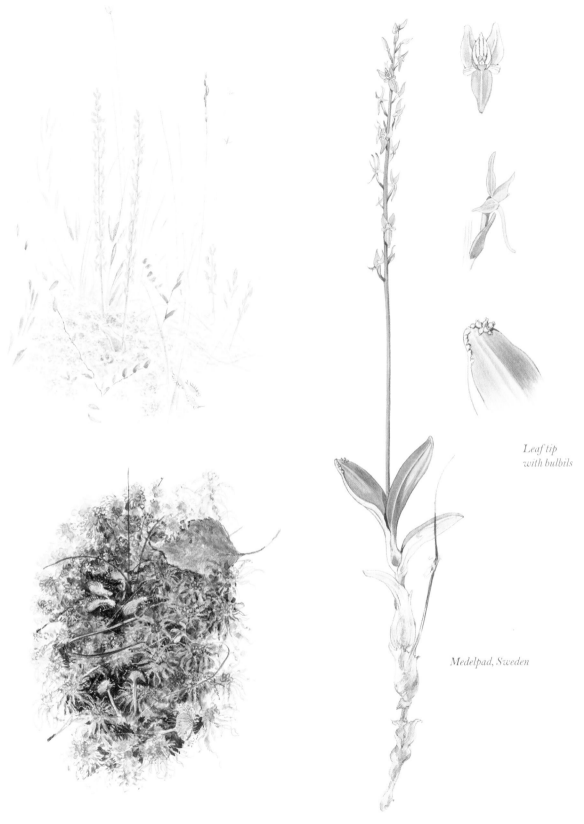

*Leaf tip
with bulbils*

Medelpad, Sweden

Hammarbya paludosa

BOG ORCHID

2–20(–25) cm; late summer; central and northern Europe (excluding Iceland),
temperate Asia and temperate North America.

Liparis

THIS GENUS ENCOMPASSES both epiphytes and terrestrial species from a broad range of environments. The sole European species is terrestrial, and it has very specific habitat requirements as it only occurs in calcareous fens and meadows – sometimes inland, sometimes in coastal dune slacks. Flowering occurs in summer.

Liparis loeselii is the only European orchid with a stem that is triangular in cross section. The European member of *Liparis* is also characterized by the combination of: (1) bracts that are less than 0.2 times as long as the stalked ovaries, (2) virtually unscented tiny flowers with the lip placed on the lower side (or nearly so), (3) spreading petals that are shorter than the sepals and (4) an abruptly recurved, oblong, rounded lip that lacks a spur and is uniformly pale green. Finally, it is worth noting that each shoot normally bears two leaves that are usually longer than 2.5 cm. Plants from coastal dune slacks between Wales and northern France have rounded (not subacute) leaves; they are often recognized as var. *ovata*.

According to recent estimates, *Liparis* counts around 320 species, and it occurs in all continents except Antarctica. However, the total distribution is somewhat fragmentary, mainly including areas in tropical Africa (with Madagascar), South-East Asia, tropical America, the eastern USA and Europe. The vast majority of species are strictly tropical.

Pollination

Liparis loeselii has a consistently high natural fruit set (*c.*80 per cent on average) that is ensured by self-pollination. The anther starts degenerating within 1–4 days after the flower has opened, and due to contraction of the dead tissue it becomes raised as a lid. When the anther is raised, the pollinia fall down and descend to the edge of the ridge-like sterile stigma part where they are usually held by a small amount of adhesive. Sometimes the pollinia rotate directly onto the fertile stigma part just below this point, but self-pollination only works efficiently if assisted by rain. When the raised anther is hit by a rain drop, it is pushed rapidly downwards, in turn knocking the pollinia over the ridge, onto the fertile stigma part. Alternatively, a rain drop may pull the pollinia to the stigma by cohesion, either as the water flows quickly over the surface of the flower, or as a drop held in the flower decreases in size by evaporation.

Öland, Sweden

*Remains of fruiting inflorescence
from the preceding year*

Liparis loeselii var. *loeselii*

FEN ORCHID

3–25 cm; summer; from Wales and France to the central Russian uplands –
and in temperate parts of eastern North America.

Malaxis

* ADDER'S MOUTHS *
Population dynamics in time and space

MALAXIS MONOPHYLLOS, the only European species of this genus, requires moist to wet, preferably basic, ground and high humidity. It thrives particularly well in alder coppices, but also grows under full exposure or partial shade in other habitats – such as fens, forest edges and stream banks. Flowering occurs in summer.

The European member of *Malaxis* is mainly characterized by the combination of: (1) bracts that are at least half as long as the stalked ovaries, (2) virtually unscented tiny flowers with the lip placed on the upper side (due to the ovary being twisted 360°), (3) recurved petals that are shorter than the sepals and (4) a straight, cordate, long-acuminate lip that lacks a spur and is uniformly pale green. It is also worth noting that each flowering shoot normally bears only a single leaf that is usually longer than 2.5 cm.

According to recent estimates, the genus counts around 300 species, most of which are restricted to tropical (or subtropical) regions. However, a few species inhabit temperate regions in Europe, Asia and North America, meaning that the total range of *Malaxis* is almost worldwide.

Population biology and pollination

Malaxis monophyllos is characterized by erratic occurrence and by dramatic fluctuations in both the size and spatial structure of local populations. Adult individuals can survive purely underground for one or more years, but it seems that underground survival is relatively infrequent and usually lasts for only one year. In Poland it has been observed that individual plants live for 1–6 years after their first appearance above ground.

The European species is mainly pollinated by fungus gnats that visit the flowers at dusk and forage on the sparse nectar secreted from the lip base.

Migration and future prospects

Patterns of genetic variation in the Old World range of *M. monophyllos* suggest that, following the last glaciation, this species expanded northwards by broad-fronted migration from at least two glacial refugia (one of which was probably the Alps). Based on modelling that combined current distribution data with scenarios of future climatic developments, it was recently predicted that by 2080 the European areas suitable for *M. monophyllos* will have been reduced significantly. In the same study, the northern to north-western part of Scandinavia was pinpointed as the most likely future core area for *M. monophyllos* in Europe.

Medelpad, Sweden

Malaxis monophyllos var. monophyllos

SINGLE–LEAVED BOG ORCHID

5–30(–50) cm; summer; from the Alps, northern and eastern Europe across (mainly temperate)
Asia to the Aleutian Islands and British Columbia.

Calypso

Deceptive 'fairies' of the conifer forest

CALYPSO MAINLY OCCURS on moist and moss-covered, humus-rich ground in old spruce forest, but it can also be found in pine woods and in nutrient-rich spruce mires. Many sites with this orchid are situated on calcareous banks on elevated sea floors, and others on terraces of basic rocks. Notwithstanding the overall habitat, *Calypso* usually grows under light shade on fairly open slopes. Flowering occurs in spring, just after the snow has melted.

This is the only European orchid genus with solitary flowers in which the spur of the lip is distinctly cleft. It is also characterized by each flowering shoot producing only one leaf (which is purple underneath) and by the flat part of the lip bearing three yellow (to cream) hair tufts at base.

The genus consists of only one species, *C. bulbosa*, with a wide distribution in the northern hemisphere. From Sweden and Finland it occurs across northern Siberia to China and Japan. In eastern North America, *Calypso* is confined to a zone along the US/Canadian border, but in the west it extends southwards in the cordillera, almost reaching Mexico.

Annual growth cycle

The inflorescence is produced from the pseudobulb in spring, and the leaf withers during fruit development in summer. This is followed by the formation of a new pseudobulb (rarely two) to replace the old one. A new leaf is produced from the young pseudobulb during autumn and lives through the winter.

Pollination

The flower of *C. bulbosa* does not produce nectar or any other pollinator reward, but it emits a sweet scent that attracts bumblebee queens (and females of parasitic bumblebee species). The visiting insect lands on the lip and inserts its head and thorax deeply into the flower to search the bottom of the spur for nectar. As the flat part of the lip is parallel to the spur, the insect must bend 180°. In doing so, it exposes a minute, hairless crevice on the rear of its thorax, and when retreating from the flower, the pollinia are attached to this exact spot by means of the viscidium. Deposition of previously acquired pollinia on the concave stigma likewise occurs when the bee leaves the flower. Individual bumblebees rapidly learn to avoid the flowers of this deceptive species. Nevertheless, the natural fruit set in European populations has been reported to vary from 21–82 per cent which is unusually high for an orchid species without pollinator reward.

Leaf seen from below

Västerbotten, Sweden

Calypso bulbosa var. *bulbosa*

CALYPSO

4–20 cm; spring; from Sweden and Finland across northern temperate Siberia
to Sakhalin, Mongolia and Korea.

Corallorhiza

* CORALROOTS *

Indirect parasites on trees

CORALLORHIZA TRIFIDA, the sole European member of this genus, usually grows on moist to wet, basic to fairly acid, moss-covered ground. It can be found in conifer forest, willow scrub and birch woods, and on north-facing slopes on heaths. Less frequently, it grows in semi-open fens or mires, or in beech woods on calcareous ground. The flowering time is spring to early summer.

Corallorhiza is easily recognized by the combination of: (1) a slender stem only provided with scale leaves, (2) spreading to suberect, tiny flowers (lateral sepals less than 7 mm long) and (3) an unspurred white lip with two short smooth ridges at the base (and often spotted violet).

Of the 11 species making up this genus, 10 are restricted to the New World where *Corallorhiza* is distributed from Alaska and Greenland to El Salvador. The total range of the genus also includes most of Europe and temperate Asia.

Mycorrhiza

Laboratory experiments using small, soil-filled glass containers with fungus-infected seedlings of *C. trifida* and young, initially fungus-free individuals of Creeping Willow (*Salix repens*) and Silver Birch (*Betula pendula*) have shown that, in a few weeks, the fungi already forming orchid mycorrhiza send out hyphae that connect with the roots of either woody plant. Here, they establish a different kind of mycorrhiza. In this way, a physiological bridge is established between the orchid and the woody plant. *Corallorhiza trifida* seedlings with a physiological bridge gain in weight, while seedlings without such a bridge actually lose weight. The experiments by McKendrick and co-workers have also documented transfer of carbon from the woody plant across the physiological bridge to the orchid. Extrapolating the laboratory results to conditions in the wild, it must be assumed that certain woody plants serve as ultimate carbon sources for the underground seedlings of *C. trifida*.

Pollination

The flowers of *C. trifida* are visited by small insects, but as the viscidium is only functional before the flower opens, insect pollination cannot play a significant role. Instead, we are dealing with a case of self-pollination. When the anther has ruptured, it lifts, dries up and is soon detached from the column. From that point the pollinia lie loose, and even a small vibration will make them fall down. Their limp, elastic stalks control the fall so that they swing onto the stigma.

Remains of fruiting
inflorescence from the
preceding year

Uppland, Sweden

Rhizome

Corallorhiza trifida

CORALROOT ORCHID

5–30 cm; spring to early summer; Arctic to temperate regions in the northern hemisphere,
and with scattered occurrences on mountains in adjoining subtropical regions.

Goodyera

Mycorrhiza of mutual benefit

THE TWO EUROPEAN species of this genus are forest plants with highly diverging habitat requirements. *Goodyera repens* grows on mossy, more or less acid ground in pine woods and open stands of spruce or fir; it occurs in plantations as well as natural forest. In contrast, *G. macrophylla* is restricted to moist ground in humid, ancient laurel forest. *Goodyera repens* blooms profusely in summer. *Goodyera macrophylla*, on the other hand, blooms in autumn – and several years may pass between each flowering event.

Goodyera is mainly characterized by the combination of: (1) reticulate-veined foliage leaves concentrated at the base of the stem, (2) a dense inflorescence of small white glandular-hairy flowers and (3) an unspurred lip with entire margins.

The genus is estimated to contain 80-100 species. The total range is mainly in the northern hemisphere and includes both temperate and tropical regions. From Europe and mainland Asia it extends southwards to Queensland and eastwards to North and Central America. Isolated occurrences are found in Mozambique and Madagascar, and on additional islands in the Indian Ocean.

Mycorrhiza

Comparison of *G. repens* seedlings grown on agar with or without the fungus *Ceratobasidium cornigerum* have shown that mycorrhiza-forming seedlings have higher growth rates and higher levels of phosphorus and nitrogen, and it has been documented that the fungus enhances nutrient uptake. In adult individuals of *G. repens*, roots and rhizomes are invariably infected by *C. cornigerum*.

In laboratory experiments where adult plants of *G. repens* and the free part of their mycorrhizal fungus were fed carbon compounds containing the isotopes ^{14}C and ^{13}C, respectively, Cameron and co-workers have demonstrated that carbon assimilated by the fungus is transferred to the orchid, but also that even higher quantities of carbon fixed by the orchid are allocated to the fungus. Although certain methodological limitations should be kept in mind, Cameron's studies are highly interesting, because they have provided the first direct evidence for mutual benefit in orchid mycorrhiza (photosynthetically fixed carbon passing from the orchid to the fungus in return for nitrogen). In all other cases of orchid mycorrhiza studied up to now, the orchid receives nourishment from the fungus without appearing to provide anything in return.

Uppland, Sweden

Goodyera repens

CREEPING LADY'S-TRESSES

(1) (5–)10–30(–40) cm; summer; cool-temperate regions
in the northern hemisphere (in Europe distributed from
Scotland and northern Scandinavia to the Pyrenees, the
Apennines and the Balkans).

Goodyera macrophylla

MADEIRAN LADY'S-TRESSES

(2) 20–60(–70) cm; autumn; Madeira.

Spiranthes

✳ LADY'S-TRESSES ✳
Natives, immigrants and aliens

THE EUROPEAN SPECIES grow at fully exposed sites. *Spiranthes spiralis* can be found on open ground in garrigue, but it mainly grows in short turf on nutrient-poor grassland; in parts of its range it is also often encountered on lawns and church yards, on golf and tennis courts, and the like. The other species of *Spiranthes* occurring in Europe grow in moist to wet places, usually fens or marshes; *S. aestivalis* requires basic, *S. romanzoffiana* acid soils. *Spiranthes spiralis* blooms from late summer to autumn, whereas the other European species are summer-flowering.

Spiranthes is mainly characterized by the combination of: (1) parallel-veined foliage leaves, (2) a dense inflorescence of white glandular-hairy flowers arranged in a spiral or in distinct rows and (3) an unspurred lip with an erose front margin.

Just about 40 species of *Spiranthes* are known globally, most of them occurring in North America. The total range of the genus additionally encompasses northern South America as well as major parts of the Mediterranean region, temperate Europe and Siberia, from where it extends across South-East Asia to eastern Australia and New Zealand.

Occurrence history

Spiranthes aestivalis and *S. spiralis* are ancient, native members of the European flora, whereas other *Spiranthes* species have a different history on this continent. *Spiranthes romanzoffiana* was unknown outside America until one occurrence was discovered in Ireland around 1810; today, scattered populations are known in the western part of the British Isles. The species was hardly cultivated in European gardens when it was first discovered in the British Isles, and it is widely accepted that it occurs naturally in this corner of Europe. The degree of genetic divergence is too little to make it probable that the species existed in the British Isles prior to the opening of the North Atlantic – modern immigration by long-distance dispersal from North America seems much more likely. The dust-like seeds allow for long-distance dispersal by wind, but alternatively it has been suggested that seeds have been transported in the plumage of migratory birds. In the last few years, four *Spiranthes* species have been newly found in the Netherlands: *S. cernua*, *S. lucida*, *S. odorata* and *S. romanzoffiana*. It is generally assumed that all of these are aliens that have escaped from cultivation in gardens.

Oregon, USA

Spiranthes romanzoffiana

IRISH LADY'S-TRESSES

10–30 cm; late summer; the British Isles, northern and western North America.

Preparatory sketches for the plate on page 71

Spiranthes romanzoffiana

IRISH LADY'S-TRESSES

data given on page 71.

Bornholm, Denmark

From herbarium specimen

Spiranthes spiralis

AUTUMN LADY'S-TRESSES

(1) 6–30(–40) cm; late summer to autumn; from Ireland and England across western, central and southern Europe to Mediterranean North Africa and south-western Asia.

Spiranthes aestivalis

SUMMER LADY'S-TRESSES

(2) 10–40 cm; summer; from western and central Europe across the western Mediterranean to Morocco, Algeria and Tunisia.

Herminium

* MUSK ORCHID & RELATIVES *
Small plants, strong scent

HERMINIUM MONORCHIS, the sole European member of this genus, can be found on fairly dry chalk grassland, but it much more frequently grows among low herbs and grasses in calcareous fens and meadows, sometimes located in coastal dune slacks. At inland sites, it seems to favour seepage water. Flowering occurs in summer.

The strongly honey-scented yellow or greenish-yellow flowers with petals longer than sepals, and with a hastate lip, distinguish *H. monorchis* from all other European orchids. The identification is further supported by the presence of 1–3(–4) green leaves that are more than 0.3 cm wide and that neither stem nor lip and petals are hairy.

Following recent systematic changes, *Herminium* is estimated to contain around 47 species. The distribution extends from Europe across temperate parts of Siberia to China, Japan and Taiwan and further south to the Himalayas, Pakistan, mainland South-East Asia and scattered areas in Malesia.

Growth and flowering

As in many other orchids with underground tubers, the old tuber is replaced annually in *H. monorchis*. Vegetative propagation is efficient in this species because not only one, but two or three new tubers are normally produced. Each new tuber is formed at the end of a runner that is usually 1–10 cm long.

The flowering rate in *H. monorchis* often fluctuates greatly among years. According to a British study, drought and high temperatures in summer probably cause premature withering of the leaves – and, hence, reduce the amount of organic matter that can be produced and stored in the new tubers. Under such conditions, the new tubers will be smaller and often unable to initiate inflorescence formation the following year.

Pollination

The remarkably powerful scent of the flowers attracts small insects, mainly flies and parasitic wasps. They usually alight on the upper half of the inflorescence, from where they run between individual flowers and enter them from above or from the side. Such individual flower visits usually last less than one minute. The insect enters the flower more or less upside down and inserts its head and front legs into the concave base of the lip where a small quantity of nectar is available. The front legs then slip into the viscidia that become attached to the thighs. During subsequent flower visits, a few pollinium fragments are deposited on the stigma in each flower.

Öland, Sweden

Herminium monorchis

MUSK ORCHID

3–30(–35) cm; summer; from England and southern Scandinavia across central
and south-eastern Europe to temperate Asia (reaching the Caucasus, Mongolia and Japan).

Habenaria

* BOG ORCHIDS *

Secrets to be revealed at night?

HABENARIA TRIDACTYLITES, the sole European species of *Habenaria*, grows in fairly dry to moist, weakly acid soil under fully exposed to partially shaded conditions. Typical habitats include rock fissures, abandoned agricultural terraces and open forest on rocky slopes. Flowering occurs from late autumn to winter.

Habenaria is the only orchid genus in Europe in which the fertile part of the stigma is divided among two freely extending branches of the column. Furthermore, *H. tridactylites* is the only European orchid that combines green or yellowish-green flower colour with a lip that is divided into three subsimilar, narrowly linear segments.

Numbering around 600 species globally, *Habenaria* is by far the largest orchid genus to be represented in Europe, where *H. tridactylites* is endemic to the Canary Islands. The complete absence of *Habenaria* from other parts of the Mediterranean region and the Middle East is surprising, given that the genus is distributed in virtually all other subtropical and tropical regions of the world (except the extremely dry ones).

Aspects of growth

The leaves of *H. tridactylites* appear some three months prior to the blooming time, and it is remarkable that they remain fresh and green for several weeks after flowering has ceased. The species often forms dense groups of plants, indicating efficient vegetative propagation. This happens when the old tuber of an individual is replaced by more than one new.

Pollination

Habenaria tridactylites is incapable of efficient self-pollination, so the consistently high natural fruit set (47–73 per cent reported from different populations) shows that suitable insect pollinators must be fairly abundant. The sweet-scented flowers with a slender, nectar-producing spur clearly suggest moth pollination. Persistent attempts at observing pollinators during day and dusk have been almost completely in vain, for which reason the species is now believed to be pollinated by moths at night-time. This assumption is supported by the fact that the only reported observation of a pollinator on *H. tridactylites* is concerned with a pollinium-bearing individual of a species of *Mamestra* (probably the Cabbage Moth, *M. brassicae*). Still, the pollination biology of the endemic *H. tridactylites* remains virtually undocumented. Who will be the first to conduct a moonlight study in the Canary Islands?

From cultivated plant

Habenaria tridactylites

THREE-LOBED HABENARIA

10–30(–60) cm; late autumn to winter; the Canary Islands.

Gennaria & Ponerorchis

G ENNARIA OCCURS on acid to slightly basic, more or less shaded ground; typical habitats include laurel forest, rock fissures and pine forest, but the sole species, *G. diphylla*, may also be found in garrigue. The only European representative of *Ponerorchis*, *P. cucullata*, requires moist, acid soil and occurs under more or less shaded conditions – mainly in conifer forest, but also in mixed or deciduous forest and in scrub. Depending on the local climatic conditions, *Gennaria* blooms during winter or spring, whereas *Ponerorchis* is consistently summer-flowering.

In *Gennaria diphylla* and *Ponerorchis cucullata* the stem is hairless and bears only two (rarely three) foliage leaves; all flowers in the inflorescence are turned towards the same side, they are yellowish-green or pink, and they have a deeply three-lobed lip with a spur. This combination of features separates the two species from all other European orchids. *Gennaria diphylla* is distinguished from *Ponerorchis cucullata* by its alternate (not basal) leaves, its yellowish-green (not pink) flowers and its cup-like (not cylindrical) spur.

Gennaria is almost entirely distributed in coastal areas of the central to western Mediterranean region, including Madeira and the Canary Islands. *Ponerorchis* (including the previously recognized *Neottianthe*) numbers *c.*50 species; it is distributed from eastern Europe to Japan and northern parts of South-East Asia.

Pollination

The flowers of *Gennaria* are spontaneously self-pollinating. In the open flower, the anther compartments are wide open. Therefore, the pollinia can easily fall out, but, as the viscidia stay in place, the pollinia will pivot onto the fertile part of the stigma immediately below.

Until now, only workers of the Common Carder Bee (*Bombus pascuorum*) have been observed as pollinators of *Ponerorchis cucullata*, but additional species of bumblebee (*Bombus*) may contribute. *Ponerorchis cucullata* exhibits delayed pollinium movement (see p. 25), which is usually an adaptation that increases the frequency of cross-pollination. However, in this species the pollinium movement takes only *c.*8 seconds, whereas most flower visits take 10–30 seconds. Thus, an acquired pollinium will normally reach a position fitting the stigma before the insect leaves the flower that donated the pollinium.

From cultivated plant

From cultivated plant

Gennaria diphylla

TWO-LEAVED GENNARIA

(1) 10–30(–50) cm; winter to spring; the Canary Islands,
Madeira and coastal regions of the western Mediterranean.

Ponerorchis cucullata

HOODED ORCHID

(2) 10–30(–40) cm; summer; from Poland to Japan
and the Himalayas.

Pseudorchis

* SMALL-WHITE ORCHID *
High fungus diversity in roots and tubers

PSEUDORCHIS ALBIDA, arguably the only species in this genus, mostly occurs in fully exposed situations in low-growing herb and grass communities in well-drained hay meadows and on grassland and heaths; occasionally, it is also encountered in marshes or fens, or even under partial shade in open woodland. *Pseudorchis albida* ssp. *albida* grows in lowland and subalpine areas, whereas ssp. *straminea* is an almost exclusively alpine plant. Flowering occurs in summer.

Pseudorchis is mainly characterized by the combination of: (1) a stem with alternating leaves and hairless, (2) tiny white to cream, vanilla-scented flowers, (3) the sepals and petals forming a hood over the column, (4) a three-lobed lip with more or less acute lobes and (5) a short spur that is somewhat constricted at the base.

The genus is distributed from Kamchatka across Siberia and central Asia to central and northern Europe. Additionally, it occurs in southern European mountains, Greenland, New Foundland and Quebec.

The two subspecies recognized here are treated as distinct species by some authors. However, whereas they are clearly genetically and structurally different in Scandinavia, they are not clearly separated in central Europe. It has been suggested that the clear distinction in Scandinavia is due to separate immigration histories for the two subspecies into Scandinavia following the last glaciation.

Root-associated fungi

In the Czech Republic, screening of *Pseudorchis* underground organs for mycorrhiza-forming and other root-associated fungi revealed no less than 66 distinct kinds – the highest number detected in a single orchid species so far. Mycorrhizal colonization of roots and tubers was found to be highest in summer, but only three species of *Tulasnella* were documented to form mycorrhiza with *Pseudorchis*. Next to nothing is known about the ecological role of the numerous other root-associated fungi.

Pollination

The characteristically vanilla-scented flowers attract a selection of insects, among which various species of smaller moths act as efficient pollinators when probing the spur for nectar. However, the *Pseudorchis* flower is also capable of spontaneous self-pollination. The anther compartments open widely, and detached pollinium fragments can fall unhindered onto the fertile stigma lobes that are situated at either side of the basal part of the anther.

Härjedalen, Sweden

Lycksele Lappmark, Sweden

Pseudorchis albida

SMALL-WHITE ORCHID

(1) ssp. *albida*; (10–)15–30 cm; summer; most of Europe (mainly excluding Iceland,
the high mountains and the Mediterranean lowland).
(2) ssp. *straminea*; 10–20(–25) cm; summer; Quebec, New Foundland, Greenland, Iceland, the Faroe Islands,
central European mountains and from Scandinavia to north-western Russia.

Platanthera

✳ BUTTERFLY-ORCHIDS ✳
Natural selection at work

TOGETHER, THE EUROPEAN species of *Platanthera* cover a very broad ecological range as they can grow in dry to moist, poor to fertile and acid to basic soil under shaded to fully exposed conditions. Depending on the species, typical habitats include marshes, heaths, woods, scrub, grassland, lower alpine heaths and late successional stages of lava fields. The flowering time is late spring to summer.

Platanthera is mainly characterized by the combination of: (1) widely spreading to reflexed lateral sepals, (2) the petals being more than half as wide as the lip, (3) a cream to pale green or yellowish-green, entire lip that is at least twice as long as wide, (4) a nectar-producing spur that is not constricted at base and (5) two freely exposed viscidia.

The total distribution of this genus, containing *c.*200 species, is very wide. It mainly encompasses subarctic, temperate and subtropical regions of the northern hemisphere, but also extends southward across tropical regions to Central America and to major parts of South-East Asia.

Pollination and spur length

All European species of *Platanthera* are either self-pollinating or pollinated by moths. Among the moth-pollinated species, *P. bifolia* exhibits an interesting variation in spur length. In this book, we tentatively treat short-spurred and long-spurred forms as ssp. *bifolia* and ssp. *latiflora*, respectively, admitting that further studies are desirable.

A transplant experiment between a long-spurred woodland population and a short-spurred alvar population of *P. bifolia* in Sweden has confirmed that the difference in spur length has a genetic basis. Thus, one year after transplantation, the plants originating from the alvar still had significantly shorter spurs at both sites. In a different study, covering several regions and habitats across Norway and Sweden, it has been demonstrated that spur length is positively related to proboscis length of the local pollinators. Variation in proboscis length within three important pollinator species was found to be very limited within and among regions and did not match variation in spur length. Therefore, it seems that current spur length in populations of *P. bifolia* has mainly evolved in response to variation in composition of the local pollinator fauna. In conclusion, the evolution of spur length is dynamic and largely driven by pollinator shifts followed by natural selection.

Iceland

Platanthera micrantha

NARROW-LIPPED BUTTERFLY-ORCHID

(1) 14–50 cm; summer; the Azores.

Platanthera pollostantha

SHORT-SPURRED BUTTERFLY-ORCHID

(2) 8–42 cm; summer; the Azores.

Platanthera hyperborea

NORTHERN BUTTERFLY-ORCHID

(3) 5–35(–45) cm; summer; Iceland and Greenland.

Torne Lappmark, Sweden

Platanthera oligantha

ONE-LEAVED BUTTERFLY-ORCHID

5–20 cm; summer; northern Scandinavia, eastern Siberia, Kamchatka and the Commander Islands.

1

2

Uppland, Sweden

Öland, Sweden

Platanthera bifolia

LESSER BUTTERFLY-ORCHID

pro parte: (1) ssp. *bifolia*; 8–35(–46) cm; summer;
distribution insufficiently known, encompassing at least
northern and north-western Europe.

Platanthera chlorantha

GREATER BUTTERFLY-ORCHID

(2) (15–)20–60(–80) cm; late spring to summer; from the
British Isles across most of Europe, the Middle East, the
Caucasus and southern temperate Asia to China and Japan.

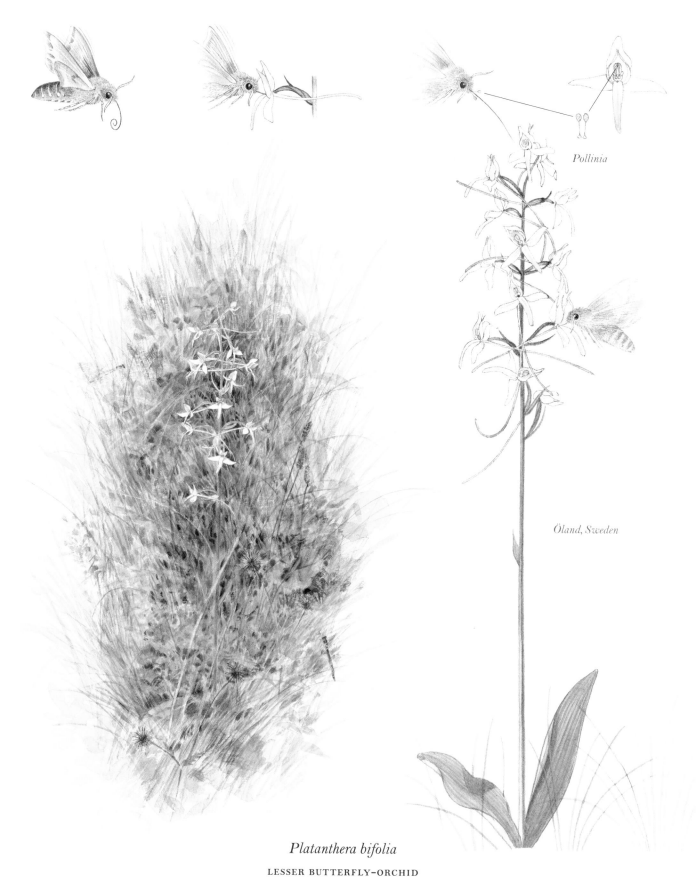

Pollinia

Öland, Sweden

Platanthera bifolia

LESSER BUTTERFLY-ORCHID

pro parte: ssp. *latiflora*; (21–)35–60(–90) cm; late spring to summer; from most of Europe to the Middle East, the Caucasus, temperate Siberia and Mongolia.

Platanthera bifolia

LESSER BUTTERFLY-ORCHID

pro parte: ssp. *latiflora*; data given on page 86.
Two-colour etching, copper graphics.

Gymnadenia

* FRAGRANT ORCHIDS *
Pollination around the clock

THE EUROPEAN SPECIES of *Gymnadenia* occur in fens, marshes and alpine meadows, and less frequently on drier grassland or on rocky slopes and cliffs with seeping water. Most members require basic soils. However, *G. frivaldii* grows in more or less neutral soil, whereas *G. conopsea* ssp. *borealis* (not illustrated in this book) is mainly a plant of poor heath soils in the British Isles and possibly elsewhere. The flowering time is early to late summer.

Gymnadenia is characterized by the combination of: (1) widely spreading to reflexed lateral sepals, (2) the petals being more than half as wide as the lip, (3) a purple to rose-coloured or pure white lip that is obscurely to distinctly three-lobed (sometimes entire in *G. frivaldii*) and usually wider than long, (4) a nectar-producing spur that is not constricted at base and (5) two freely exposed viscidia.

With the species delimitation preferred by us, *Gymnadenia* contains eight species. It occurs in most of Europe, from where the distribution extends further east across temperate Asia to Japan. Three species are known from Europe (where some botanists prefer to recognize the three subspecies of *G. conopsea* as species in their own right).

Pollination

The vast majority of orchids and other insect-pollinated plants have specialized on pollinators operating at either day- or night-time, but this is not the case with *G. conopsea*. Scent emission in this species is particularly strong at dusk, and moths operating in the dark hours are usually the most important pollinators. However, butterflies operating during the day normally pollinate about 25 per cent of the flowers, and populations are known where they are more important pollinators than moths. The flowers are clearly adapted to pollination by moths and butterflies, as these are the only European insects with sufficiently long mouthparts to reach to the bottom of the long, slender spur. However, an interesting case has been reported from the Netherlands where two bumblebee species at one site, and in just one season, exploited the nectar in the upper part of the *G. conopsea* spur; during their flower visits, they acted as highly efficient pollinators.

Gymnadenia odoratissima is likewise mainly pollinated by butterflies and moths in varying proportions (with minor contributions from certain beetles and flies). The pollination biology of *G. frivaldii* is virtually unknown.

The Transsylvanian Alps, Romania

Gymnadenia frivaldii

FRIVALD'S ORCHID

(together with *Pseudorchis albida*, the two plants to the right); 10–30 cm; summer;
the Balkans and the Southern Carpathians.

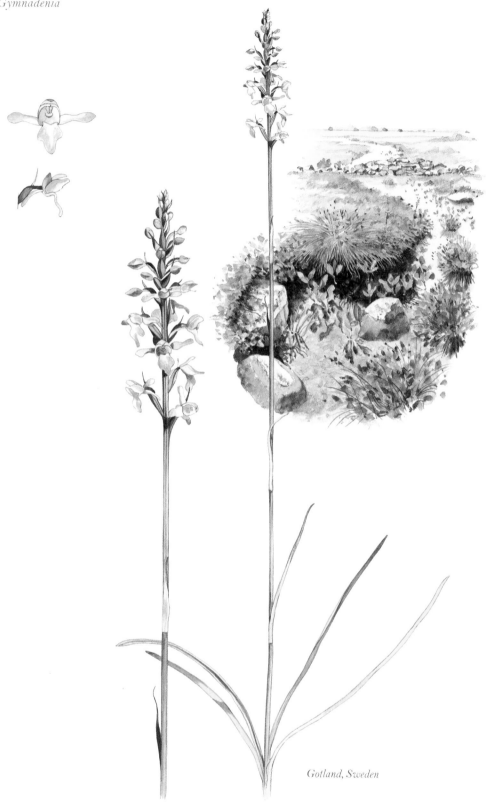

Gotland, Sweden

Gymnadenia odoratissima

SHORT-SPURRED FRAGRANT ORCHID

12–50 cm; summer; scattered from the Pyrenees across central Europe to the Balkans,
eastern Europe and the Baltic region.

1

2

Öland, Sweden

Gymnadenia conopsea

FRAGRANT ORCHID

(1) ssp. *conopsea*; 12–60 cm; summer; most of Europe and across temperate Asia to Japan and southern China.
(2) ssp. *densiflora*; 27–100 cm; late summer; scattered in major parts of Europe, but distribution insufficiently known.

Nigritella

✻ VANILLA ORCHIDS ✻

Propagation by virgin birth

THE SPECIES OF THIS genus inhabit grassland and fairly dry meadows in the montane to alpine zone, where they grow in basic soils under fully exposed conditions. Flowering occurs in summer.

Nigritella can be recognized from the following combination of features: (1) leaves several, very narrow (to about twice as wide as the stem is thick), mostly channelled; (2) inflorescence hemispherical to ovoid, very dense; (3) lip entire, placed on the upper side of the flower (due to the ovary not being twisted) and (4) the base of the lip enveloping the column (sometimes incompletely so).

According to recent estimates, this genus contains around 15 species, but most of them are extremely closely related. *Nigritella* is endemic to Europe where it occurs in the Alps, Pyrenees, Carpathians and Apennines as well as in Cordillera Cantabrica and in the mountains of Scandinavia and the Balkan Peninsula.

Diploid and polyploid species

Individuals of most plant species are diploid, that is they have two sets of chromosomes in each vegetative cell, and when generative cells are produced through division, each pollen and egg cell will only contain one chromosome set. However, some species are polyploid, which means their individuals have more than two chromosome sets in the vegetative cells. This condition may occur through accidental increase in the species itself, or it can happen in connection with hybridization where chromosome sets from different species are combined. Depending on the number of chromosome sets and their origin, polyploid species are capable or incapable of normal sexual reproduction.

Reproduction and species formation

Nigritella contains a few diploid species that are pollinated by insects and reproduce sexually. However, most members of the genus, including the two species depicted in this book, are polyploid and are incapable of sexual reproduction. Instead, they propagate by 'virgin birth' as they develop seeds without fertilization. In this way, the genes of the mother plant are transferred directly to the progeny without any recombination, meaning that mutations (fortuitous gene changes) will gradually accumulate in different breeding lines, making the lines very slightly genetically and structurally different from each other. According to tradition, such slightly diverging lines are treated as distinct species, but they are hardly comparable to species of sexually reproducing plants.

Jämtland, Sweden

Nigritella nigra

VANILLA ORCHID

(5–)9–20(–27) cm; summer; central Sweden, and central and northern Norway.

Nigritella nigra,
Vanilla Orchid, in its natural habitat.
Jämtland, Sweden

*The Transsylvanian Alps,
Romania*

Nigritella miniata

RED VANILLA ORCHID

10–30 cm; summer; the Southern Carpathians, and the central and south-eastern Alps.

Gymnigritella

* RUNE'S VANILLA ORCHID *

A genus of hybrid origin

THE SOLE SPECIES of *Gymnigritella* is a plant of grassland, marshes and heaths of Mountain Avens (*Dryas octopetala*) in the montane to lower alpine zone, where it grows in basic soil under fully exposed conditions. Flowering occurs in summer. *Gymnigritella* can be recognized from the following combination of features: (1) leaves several, very narrow (to about twice as wide as the stem is thick), mostly channelled, (2) inflorescence hemispherical to ovoid, very dense, (3) lip entire, placed on the upper side of the flower (due to the ovary not being twisted) and (4) the base of the lip not enveloping the column.

For technical reasons, a number of fortuitous species-level hybrids between *Gymnadenia* and *Nigritella* have been named under *Gymnigritella*. The only real species belonging to this genus, *G. runei*, is endemic to a small area in northern Sweden.

Evolutionary origin

Nigritella nigra is one of those polyploid *Nigritella* species that produce viable seeds without fertilization (see p. 92). Nevertheless, its flowers are sometimes visited by insects – and it appears that, in one case, a pollinator (probably a butterfly) has performed cross-pollination between *N. nigra* and *Gymnadenia conopsea*. This hybridization event led to the origin of *Gymnigritella runei*. Most individuals of *Gymnadenia conopsea* have 40 chromosomes in each vegetative cell and produce pollen and egg cells with 20 chromosomes each. *Nigritella nigra*, on the other hand, has 60 chromosomes in each vegetative cell. *Gymnigritella runei* contains 80 chromosomes in each vegetative cell, so it seems reasonable to assume that this chromosome number has been brought about by a normal pollen or egg cell from *Gymnadenia conopsea* being united with an unreduced cell from *Nigritella nigra*. Indeed, genetic studies have demonstrated that each vegetative cell in *Gymnigritella runei* contains one chromosome set from *Gymnadenia conopsea* and three sets from *Nigritella nigra*. This overrepresentation of *Nigritella* chromosomes could well explain why the visual appearance of *Gymnigritella runei* is much closer to *Nigritella nigra* than to *Gymnadenia conopsea*. Like *Nigritella nigra*, *Gymnigritella runei* is incapable of normal sexual reproduction, so it has to rely entirely on seed development without fertilization.

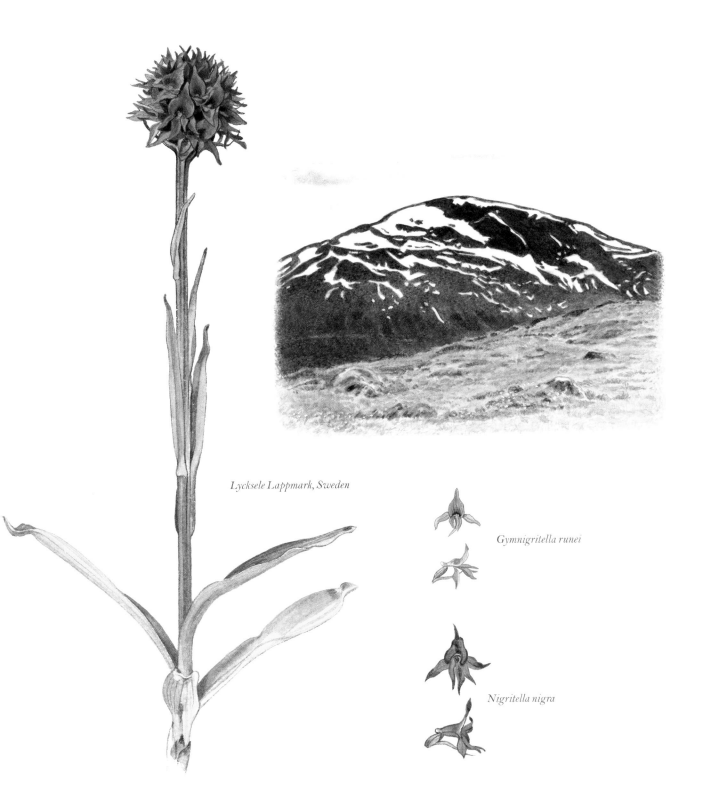

Lycksele Lappmark, Sweden

Gymnigritella runei

Nigritella nigra

Gymnigritella runei

RUNE'S VANILLA ORCHID

(with flowers of *Nigritella nigra* for comparison); 10–21 cm; summer; northern Sweden.

Coeloglossum

* FROG ORCHID *
To be or not to be (a genus)

THE ONLY SPECIES constituting this genus grows in neutral to basic soils under fully exposed to partially shaded conditions. It occurs in an extraordinarily wide range of habitats from sea level to 2900 m altitude – including, for example: grassland, heaths, meadows, scrub, fens and open woodland. Flowering occurs between late spring and late summer, depending on the local climatic conditions.

The following combination of features distinguishes *Coeloglossum* from all other European orchids: (1) flowers green or yellowish green to brown or reddish brown, (2) sepals and petals forming a hood over the column, (3) lip elongate, ending in three small teeth and (4) lip hairless, provided with a very short sac-like spur that is pressed against the flat part of the lip.

The geographic range of *Coeloglossum* encompasses nearly all of Europe (mainly excepting subtropical lowland regions) and extends across temperate Asia to North America where the genus mainly occurs in Canada and the northern USA.

Systematic position

Coeloglossum evidently has very close relations to *Dactylorhiza*, but the DNA-based studies conducted up until now have given conflicting results as to exactly how close the relationship is. Depending on the DNA region sequenced, studies have either suggested that the two genera are each other's closest relative, or that *Coeloglossum viride* originated within *Dactylorhiza*. Favouring the latter result, and arguing that genera with only one species do not convey any real information about relationships, quite a number of botanists now classify *Coeloglossum viride* in *Dactylorhiza* (under the name *D. viridis*). Accordingly, they include *Coeloglossum* as a synonym under *Dactylorhiza*. However, due to the marked differences in flower structure between *Dactylorhiza* (as delimited in this book) and *Coeloglossum*, the latter practice renders it virtually impossible to recognize *Dactylorhiza* as one unit without the aid of DNA-based methods. Under these circumstances, we think that it makes more sense to recognize a genus with just one species (a practice that, ironically, is widely accepted in many other cases). It must be hoped that more comprehensive DNA-based studies will clarify the systematic relationships in this group in the foreseeable future.

Lycksele Lappmark, Sweden

Öland, Sweden

Coeloglossum viride

FROG ORCHID

5–40 cm; late spring to summer; temperate to subarctic areas in the northern hemisphere –
and with scattered occurrences on mountains in adjoining subtropical regions.

Dactylorhiza

* MARSH-ORCHIDS & SPOTTED-ORCHIDS *
Complicated relationships

ACTYLORHIZA AS A WHOLE covers a very broad ecological range as the plants grow in dry to moist, poor to fertile, acid to basic soil under shaded to fully exposed conditions. Considering this in combination with the high number of European representatives, it is hardly surprising that the genus can be encountered in virtually any natural or semi-natural vegetation type in Europe – only avoiding saline, higher alpine and exceptionally dry environments. The flowering time is spring to summer.

Dactylorhiza can be recognized by the following combination of features: (1) not all flowers of the inflorescence turned towards the same side, (2) bracts herbaceous, not pressed against the ovaries, (3) lateral sepals widely spreading to reflexed, (4) petals less than half as wide as the lip and (5) lip hairless, provided with a spur that is not pressed against the flat part of the lip.

Species delimitation is much debated. Personally, we consider most of the variation to occur below species level, for which reason we only recognize around 15 species. The total distribution of the genus encompasses all of Europe and the Mediterranean region, from where it extends across temperate Asia to the Himalayas, Japan and Alaska.

This genus contains both diploid and polyploid species; the latter are either triploid or tetraploid, that is containing either three or four chromosome sets in each vegetative cell. Here follows a slightly simplified outline of the relationships. Among the European members, D. incarnata, D. iberica, D. sambucina, D. romana, D. maculata ssp. fuchsii, D. maculata ssp. saccifera and D. foliosa are diploid. The polyploid D. maculata ssp. maculata combines four 'fuchsii' chromosome sets in each vegetative cell, implying that it has originated directly from D. maculata ssp. fuchsii. All the remaining species in Europe are likewise polyploid, but differ in being of hybrid origin. The triploid D. insularis combines one 'sambucina' with two 'romana' chromosome sets, and it is the only Dactylorhiza that produces seed without fertilization. Dactylorhiza cantabrica is tetraploid, combining two 'sambucina' and two 'romana' chromosome sets. Finally, the tetraploid D. majalis combines two 'fuchsii' and two 'incarnata' chromosome sets. The various subspecies of D. majalis partly reflect differences in age and geographic origin.

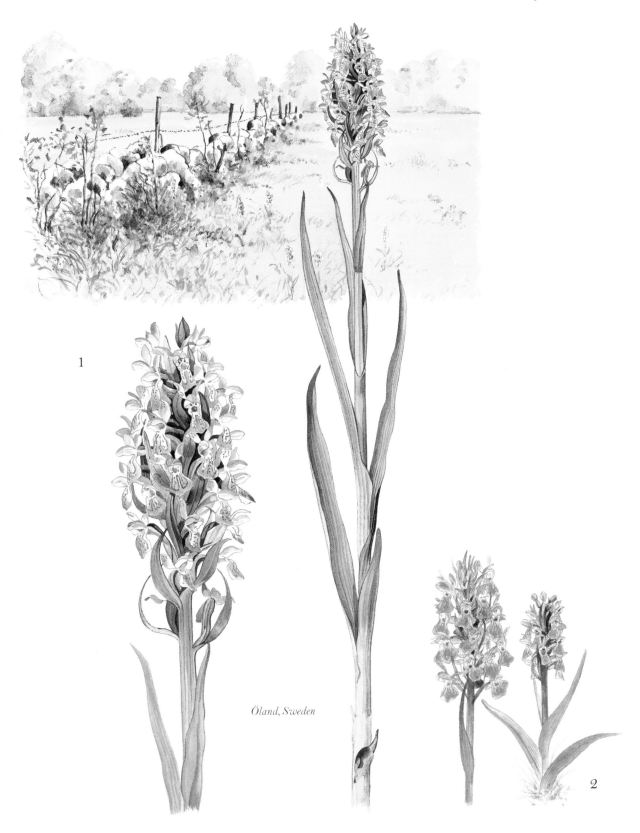

Öland, Sweden

Dactylorhiza incarnata

EARLY MARSH-ORCHID

pro parte. (1) var. *incarnata*; 15–80 cm; late spring to summer; from most of Europe to Siberia, Anatolia and central Asia.
(2) var. *coccinea*; 6–18(–25) cm; summer; the British Isles and the North Sea coast of the Netherlands,
Denmark and southern Norway.

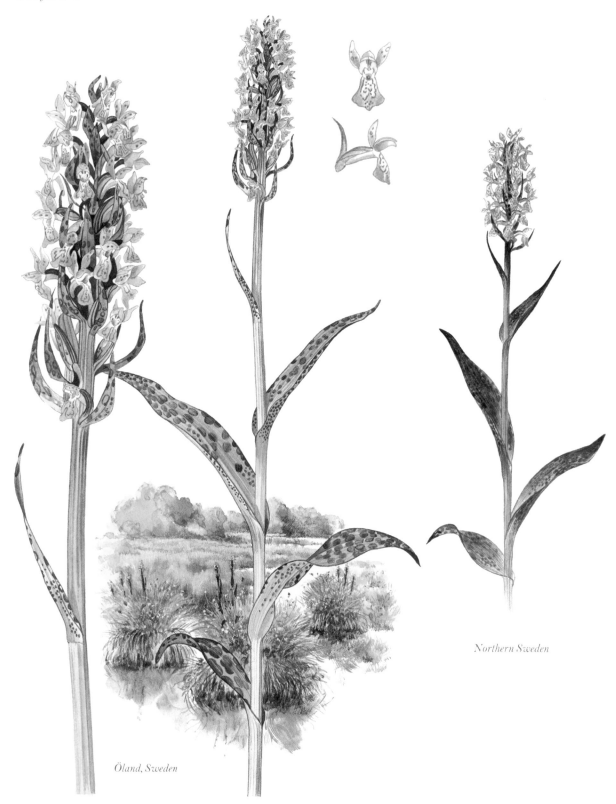

Öland, Sweden

Northern Sweden

Dactylorhiza incarnata

EARLY MARSH-ORCHID

pro parte: var. *cruenta*; 15–35(–50) cm; late spring to summer; distribution insufficiently known,
apparently scattered in major parts of temperate Europe and across Siberia to north-western China.

1

2

Öland, Sweden

Öland, Sweden

Dactylorhiza incarnata

EARLY MARSH-ORCHID

pro parte. (1) var. *ochroleuca*; 30–60(–90) cm; late spring to summer; from central Europe to England,
Gotland and Estonia. (2) var. *cruenta* × var. *ochroleuca*.

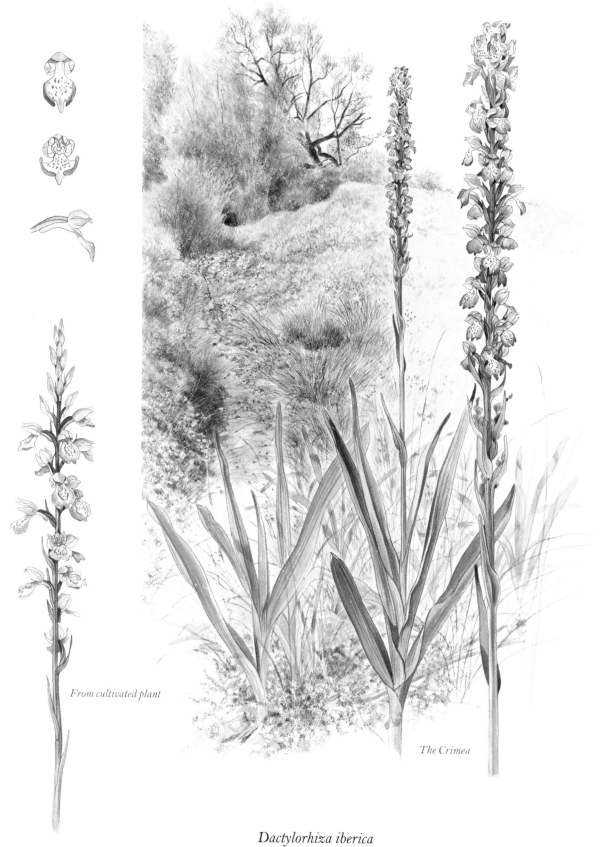

From cultivated plant

The Crimea

Dactylorhiza iberica

CRIMEAN MARSH–ORCHID

20–60 cm; summer; from Iran and the Caucasus across south-western Asia to Greece and the Crimea.

Stockholm's skerries,
Sweden

1

2

Dactylorhiza sambucina

ELDER-FLOWERED ORCHID

(1) 9–30(–45) cm; spring to early summer; most of central,
southern and south-eastern Europe – and with an isolated
area from Denmark to southern Norway, eastern Sweden
and the east coast of the Baltic Sea.

Dactylorhiza cantabrica

GALICIAN ORCHID

(2) 10–20 cm; spring; north-western Spain.

Stockholm's skerries, Sweden

Dactylorhiza sambucina

ELDER-FLOWERED ORCHID

data given on page 105.

Monte Gargano, Italy

Dactylorhiza insularis

BARTON'S ORCHID

(1) (11–)17–50 cm; spring to early summer; northern Morocco and south-western Europe (east to the west coast of mainland Italy).

Dactylorhiza romana ssp. romana

ROMAN ORCHID

(2) (7–)13–35(–50) cm; spring; from Sicily across mainland Italy, the southern Balkans, the Greek islands and Anatolia to Cyprus, Lebanon and the Crimea.

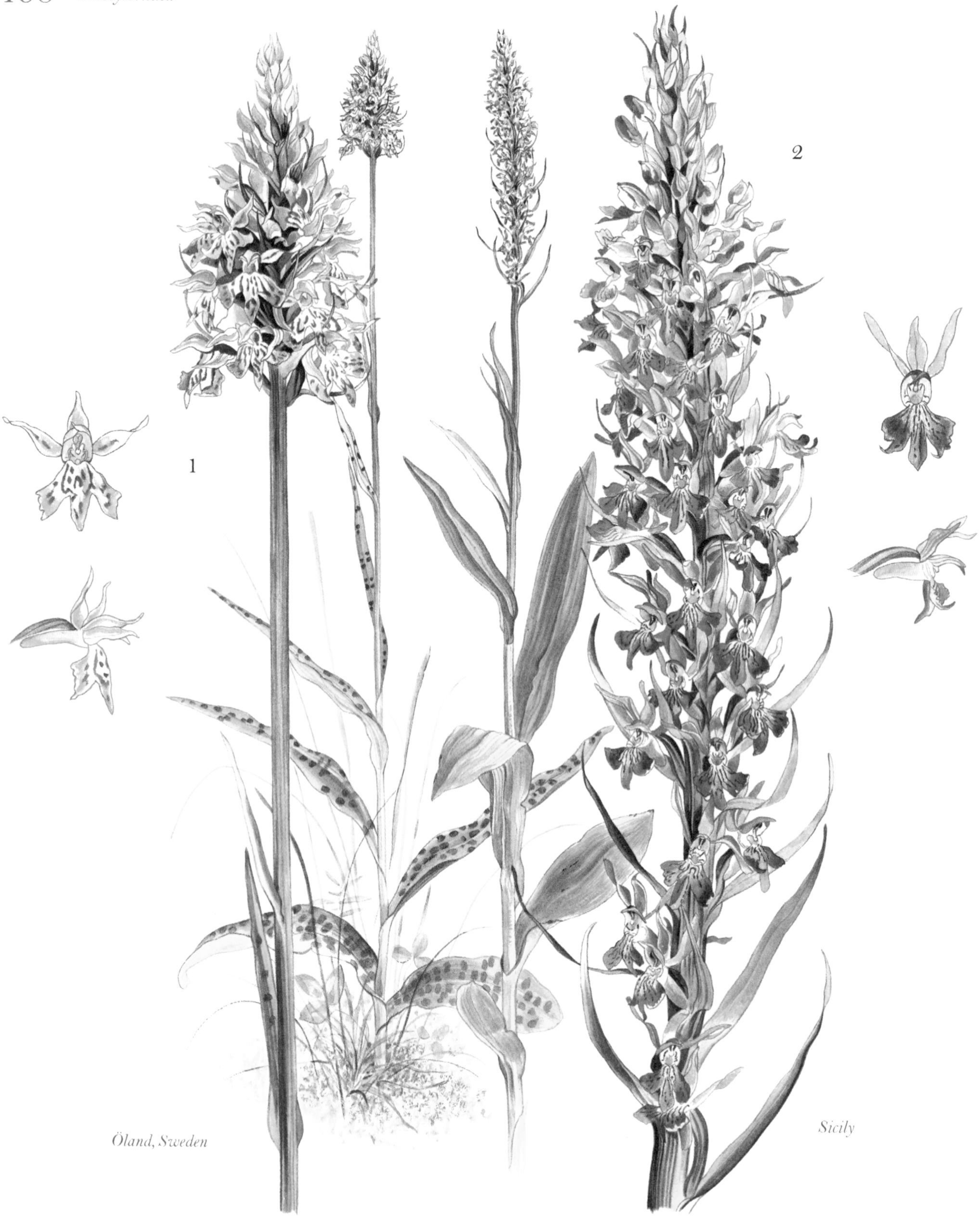

1

2

Öland, Sweden

Sicily

Dactylorhiza maculata

HEATH SPOTTED-ORCHID

pro parte. (1) ssp. *fuchsii*; (5–)15–50(–70) cm; summer; from most of Europe across Siberia to Mongolia.
(2) ssp. *saccifera*; 25–90 cm; late summer; from Corsica, Sardinia and Sicily across mainland Italy
and the Balkans to Anatolia.

1

1

1

Kent, England

2

Söndermanland, Sweden

Härjedalen, Sweden

Madeira

Dactylorhiza maculata

HEATH SPOTTED-ORCHID

pro parte: (1) ssp. *maculata*; 5–60 cm; summer; from
most of Europe to north-western Africa (Morocco,
Algeria) and central Siberia.

Dactylorhiza foliosa

MADEIRAN ORCHID

(2) 30–70 cm; late spring to summer; Madeira.

Skåne, Sweden

Dactylorhiza majalis

BROAD–LEAVED MARSH–ORCHID

pro parte: ssp. *majalis*; 10–40(–70) cm; spring to summer; central Europe to Denmark, southern Sweden
and Poland in the north, and to northern Spain, northern Italy and the north-western Balkans in the south.

The Transsylvanian Alps, Romania

Dactylorhiza majalis

BROAD–LEAVED MARSH–ORCHID

pro parte: ssp. *cordigera*; 10–40 cm; late spring to summer; from Albania
and northern Greece to the Ukraine.

Sierra Nevada, Spain

Dactylorhiza majalis

BROAD-LEAVED MARSH-ORCHID

pro parte: ssp. *sesquipedalis*; 20–125 cm; late spring to summer; south-western France and the western part of
the Mediterranean region (east to Corsica and Tunisia) – and with an isolated occurrence in the Netherlands.

1

2

Kent, England

Dactylorhiza majalis

BROAD-LEAVED MARSH-ORCHID

pro parte. (1) ssp. *integrata* var. *integrata*; 20–70(–90) cm; summer; Wales, England and the north-western part of mainland Europe.
(2) ssp. *integrata* var. *junialis*; 20–70(–90) cm; summer; England and the north-western part of mainland Europe.

Jutland, Denmark

2

Remains of fruiting inflorescence from the preceding year

Dactylorhiza majalis

BROAD-LEAVED MARSH-ORCHID

pro parte. (1) ssp. *purpurella* var. *pulchella*; (8–)13–25(–45) cm; summer; the British Isles, Denmark, western to southern Norway and the Faroe Islands. (2) ssp. *purpurella* var. *cambrensis*; (6–)13–35(–47) cm; summer; Scotland, Northern Ireland, Wales and Denmark.

Härjedalen, Sweden

Dactylorhiza majalis

BROAD-LEAVED MARSH-ORCHID

pro parte: ssp. *lapponica*; 10–30(–45) cm; summer; the British Isles, central Europe –
and from Scandinavia to the Baltic states and north-western Russia.

Medelpad, Sweden

Lycksele Lappmark, Sweden

Dactylorhiza majalis

BROAD-LEAVED MARSH-ORCHID

pro parte: ssp. *lapponica*; data given on page 115.

Estonia

1

2

Dactylorhiza majalis

BROAD-LEAVED MARSH-ORCHID

pro parte. (1) ssp. *baltica*; 25–70 cm; summer; from the southern and eastern Baltic coast to Kazakhstan – and with an isolated occurrence in northern Sweden. (2) ssp. *calcifugiens*; (9–)14–24(–34) cm; summer; north-western Denmark.

Småland, Sweden

Dactylorhiza majalis

BROAD-LEAVED MARSH-ORCHID

pro parte: ssp. *sphagnicola*; (15–)20–40(–60) cm; summer; scattered from north-eastern France
to southern Scandinavia.

Södermanland, Sweden

Dactylorhiza majalis

BROAD–LEAVED MARSH–ORCHID

pro parte: ssp. *sphagnicola*; data given on page 118.

Chamorchis

✳ FALSE MUSK ORCHID ✳
A rare case of ant pollination

THE ONLY SPECIES OF *Chamorchis* (*C. alpina*) is restricted to calcareous grassland and heaths of Mountain Avens (*Dryas octopetala*) in the alpine and upper subalpine zones. It particularly often grows under harsh conditions in the patchy vegetation of mountain summits and other rocky terrain, in central Europe often accompanied by the charismatic Edelweiss (*Leontopodium alpinum*). Flowering occurs in summer.

The genus is easily recognized by the following combination of features: (1) whole plant hairless, (2) leaves several, very narrow (to about as wide as the stem is thick), (3) flowers yellowish-green to brownish and (4) lip entire and not provided with a spur.

Chamorchis is widespread in the Scandinavian mountain chain, whereas two old occurrences in the Kola Peninsula, close to the Norwegian border, are now considered lost, meaning the genus has been extirpated in Russia. Outside the northern range, the distribution only includes the Alps and the Northern and Southern Carpathians.

Vegetative reproduction

At the time of flowering, each plant has two underground tubers: a brown, shortly stalked and contracted one that has supported early growth of the flowering shoot, and a whitish and fleshy one that is being built to store nourishment during the following winter. Vegetative reproduction often happens by the formation of two new tubers rather than one.

Pollination

At some sites, *C. alpina* is mainly pollinated by beetles and parasitic wasps. However, if the orchid is growing in the vicinity of one or more nests of a suitable ant species, it is almost exclusively ant-pollinated (wasps and beetles probably keeping away to avoid the predatory ants). This phenomenon is interesting, because ant pollination is otherwise rare – not only in orchids, but in flowering plants in general.

An insect visiting the flower will assume a longitudinal position on the lip and forage on nectar produced in its median furrow while moving upwards. When reaching the base of the lip, the insect turns either right or left in order to access additional nectar at either side of the cavity with the stigma. In doing so, it will deposit any previously acquired pollinium on the stigma, and when the insect touches one of the liquid-filled pouches on the column, a new pollinium will be attached to its head. Fruit set in *C. alpina* is usually very high, *c.*75 per cent on average.

The illustrator (B. Mossberg) painting C. alpina, *Härjedalen, Sweden*

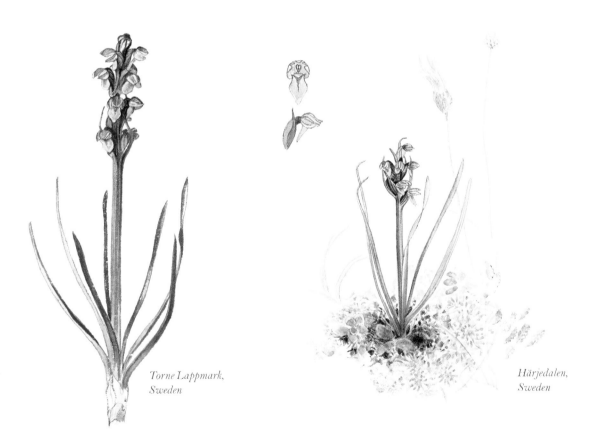

Torne Lappmark,
Sweden

Härjedalen,
Sweden

Chamorchis alpina

FALSE MUSK ORCHID

3–15 cm; summer; the Scandinavian mountain range, the Alps and the Northern and Southern Carpathians.

Traunsteinera

✳ GLOBE ORCHIDS ✳
Orchids on the roof of Europe

THE MEMBERS OF this genus are true mountain plants. *Traunsteinera globosa*, the only European species, never occurs below 500 m altitude, and the vast majority of populations are found in the range from 1000–2700 m. *Traunsteinera* thrives in fully exposed vegetation on basic to neutral ground; it mostly grows on grassland and in fairly dry meadows, less frequently in mires or gaps in pine forest. Flowering occurs in summer.

In *Traunsteinera*, the sepals and petals are prolonged into slender, club-like processes – a feature that is unique among European orchids. *Nigritella* and *Gymnigritella* have a similarly short and dense-flowered inflorescence, but they have narrower leaves, lack the club-like processes of sepals and petals and have the lip placed on the upper (rather than lower) side of the flower.

Just two species make up this genus. Their combined distribution encompasses mountains of central and south-central Europe (west to the Pyrenees) and extends eastwards across the Crimea and Anatolia to the Caucasus.

Altitudinal distribution

Traunsteinera is not the only orchid genus with populations occurring above 2,500 m altitude in Europe; the same is true for *Dactylorhiza* and *Nigritella* (to 2,600 m), *Chamorchis*, *Gymnadenia*, *Orchis* and *Pseudorchis* (to 2,700 m) and *Coeloglossum* (to 2,900 m). Among these, *Chamorchis* and *Nigritella* correspond to *Traunsteinera* in being largely restricted to the alpine and upper montane zones. However, unlike *Traunsteinera*, their distributions include northern Scandinavia where the vegetation zones concerned are found at much lower altitudes than in central Europe. Thus, *Traunsteinera* is the only European orchid genus that is largely restricted to high altitudes.

Pollination

No nectar is produced in the slender spur, and the flowers are pollinated through deceit. It has been suggested that *T. globosa* specifically mimics the inflorescences of Mountain Valerian (*Valeriana montana*), Small Scabious (*Scabiosa columbaria*) and Wood Scabious (*Knautia sylvatica*). However, no positive relationship has been demonstrated between the presence of either alleged model species and the fruit set of *T. globosa*. Therefore, rather than being a case of Batesian floral mimicry, *T. globosa* is probably pollinated through generalized food deception. The system is operated by a variety of insects – mainly flies, butterflies and moths, but also by bees and beetles.

The Transsylvanian Alps, Romania

Traunsteinera globosa

GLOBE ORCHID

20–70 cm; summer; scattered from the Pyrenees to the Caucasus
(between southern Germany in the north and the Balkans in the south).

Orchis

The genus that shrank

TOGETHER, THE EUROPEAN species of *Orchis* cover a broad ecological range as they can grow in dry to moist, fertile to fairly poor, basic to slightly acid soil under shaded to fully exposed conditions. Depending on the species, typical habitats may include garrigue, scrub, grassland, wooded meadows, woodland and subalpine meadows. The flowering time is mainly spring to summer, but with some populations of *O. patens* ssp. *canariensis* blooming as early as winter.

Orchis consistently has a hairless stem, several leaves, membranous bracts and an entire or three-lobed lip with the apical part often being cleft or incised. Its members share many traits with representatives of *Anacamptis* and *Neotinea*, but can be recognized by the combination of nearly all leaves being assembled in a basal rosette (usually less than three leaves are placed higher up on the stem), a rather lax inflorescence of small to fairly large flowers and a lip with or without tiny tufts of coloured hairs.

Today, only *c.*20 species are assigned to *Orchis*, which has its centre of diversity in Europe, the Mediterranean region and the Middle East (to Iran and the Caspian Sea). From eastern Europe, the total distribution extends further east in a narrow band across most of temperate Asia.

Just a couple of decades ago, *Orchis* was still considered a much larger genus than today. However, DNA-based studies published from the late 1990s onwards have strongly indicated that not all species traditionally assigned to *Orchis* are more closely related to each other than to members of other traditionally recognized genera. Consequently, to achieve a classification that better reflects inferred patterns of relationships, quite a number of species have recently been transferred from *Orchis* to *Anacamptis*, and a few from *Orchis* to *Neotinea* (until that point, *Anacamptis* and *Neotinea* were considered to contain only one species each). In contrast, the previously recognized genus *Aceras* (containing only *A. anthropophorum*) became included in *Orchis*. The transfers to *Anacamptis* and *Neotinea* amply outweigh the latter addition, meaning that the genus *Orchis* has shrunk considerably in recent years. It is reassuring to note that the DNA-based reclassification implies that previously confusing patterns of chromosome numbers and hybridization in this complex now make much better sense.

Castel Forte, Italy

Orchis italica

NAKED MAN ORCHID

20–50(–70) cm; spring; the Mediterranean region – except France,
Sardinia and eastern North Africa.

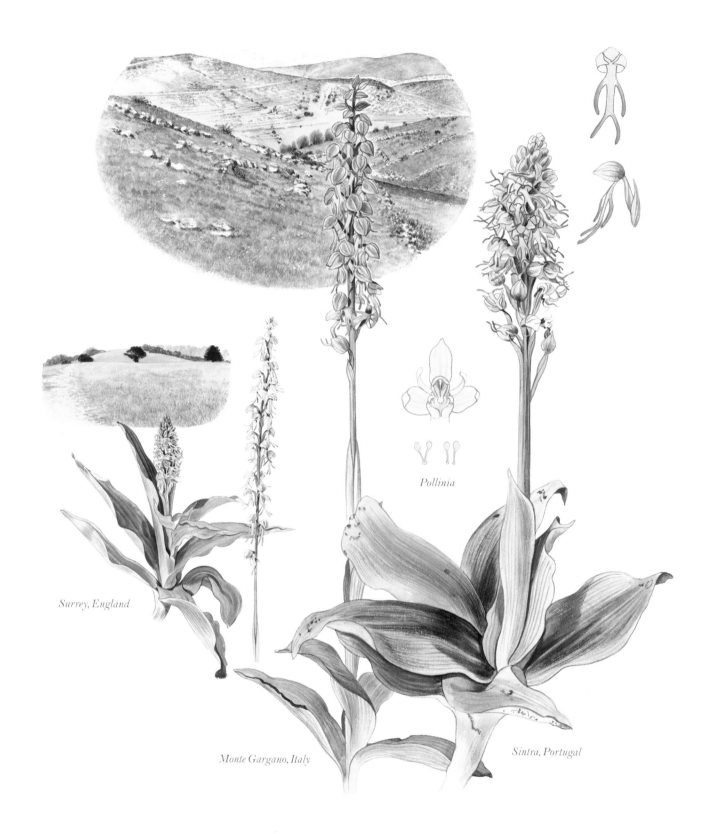

Surrey, England

Monte Gargano, Italy

Pollinia

Sintra, Portugal

Orchis anthropophora

MAN ORCHID

10–50 cm; spring to early summer; southern and western Europe (north to England),
western Mediterranean North Africa, Cyprus and southern Anatolia.

The Crimea

Orchis punctulata

PUNCTATE ORCHID

25–70(–90) cm; early spring to early summer; from south-western Asia
to the Crimea and easternmost Greece.

Møn, Denmark

Orchis purpurea ssp. *purpurea*

LADY ORCHID

15–90 cm; spring to early summer; central and southern Europe,
Anatolia and north–eastern Algeria.

Orchis militaris ssp. *militaris*

MILITARY ORCHID

20–65 cm; spring to early summer; Europe (except the northernmost and southernmost parts)
and across western Asia to the Caucasus and central Siberia.

Öland, Sweden

Öland, Sweden

Orchis militaris ssp. *militaris*

MILITARY ORCHID

data given on page 129.

San Marino

Orchis simia

MONKEY ORCHID

20–45(–60) cm; spring to early summer; from south-western Asia across southern Europe to most of France
and neighbouring regions (including England) – and with isolated occurrences in Mediterranean North Africa.

Öland, Sweden

Orchis mascula

EARLY–PURPLE ORCHID

pro parte: ssp. *mascula*; (9–)15–65 cm; spring to early summer; most of Europe (including the Canary Islands), western Mediterranean North Africa and western Asia.

Recco, Italy

Öland, Sweden

Orchis mascula

EARLY-PURPLE ORCHID

pro parte. (1) ssp. *mascula*; data given on page 132;
(2) ssp. *speciosa*; 15–60 cm; late spring to summer; the
Balkans, the Alps, the Carpathians and adjoining regions.

Orchis olbiensis

SOUTHERN EARLY-PURPLE ORCHID

(3) 10–25(–35) cm; spring; western part of the
Mediterranean region (east to Corsica and Tunisia).

Monte Gargano, Italy

Orchis provincialis

PROVENCE ORCHID

(1) 15–35 cm; spring to early summer; southern Europe and Anatolia.

Orchis pauciflora

SPARSE-FLOWERED ORCHID

(2) 10–30 cm; spring; south-eastern Europe (from Corsica to Greece).

The Crimea

Orchis pallens

PALE-FLOWERED ORCHID

15–40 cm; spring; from central and southern Europe
to south-western Asia.

Orchis patens

GREEN-SPOTTED ORCHID

(1) ssp. *patens*; 25–50(–70) cm; spring to early summer; northern Algeria, northern Tunisia and the Mediterranean coast of north-western Italy. (2) ssp. *canariensis*; 15–60 cm; winter to spring; the Canary Islands.

Recco, Italy

Gotland, Sweden

Orchis spitzelii

SPITZEL'S ORCHID

(1) ssp. *spitzelii*; 16–40(–60) cm; spring to early summer; scattered from south-western Asia across the Mediterranean region to central Europe – and with an isolated occurrence on Gotland. (2) ssp. *nitidifolia*; 15–40 cm; late spring; Crete.

1

Crete

2

Orchis anatolica

ANATOLIAN ORCHID

(1) 10–50 cm; spring; from eastern Greece across Anatolia
to Cyprus and the Middle East.

Orchis sitiaca

CRETAN ORCHID

(2) 8–50 cm; spring; Crete.

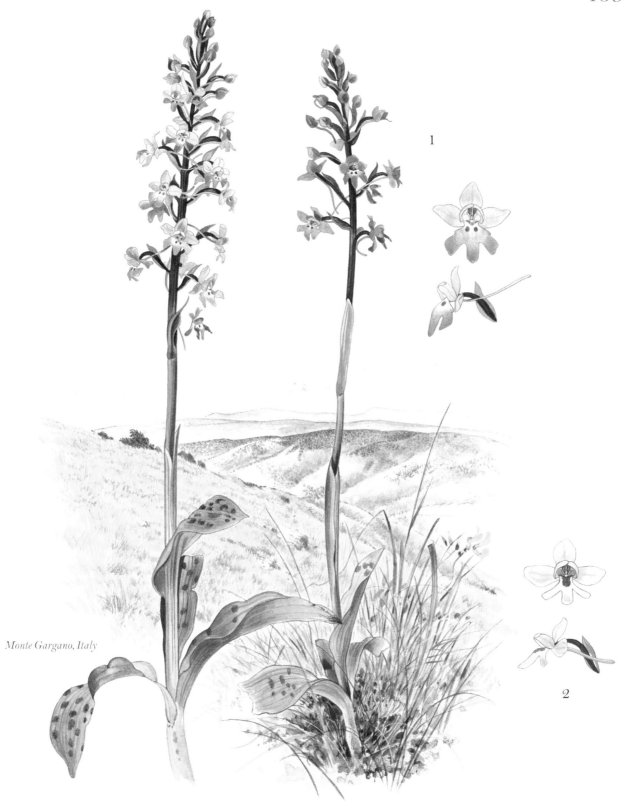

1

2

Monte Gargano, Italy

Orchis quadripunctata

FOUR-SPOTTED ORCHID

(1) 10–30(–40) cm; spring; south-eastern Europe and
north-westernmost Anatolia.

Orchis brancifortii

BRANCIFORTI'S ORCHID

(2) 10–25 cm; spring; Sardinia, Sicily and Calabria.

Neotinea

A bashful orchid and its charming relatives

S PECIES OF THIS GENUS are primarily encountered in grassland and garrigue on calcareous ground, but they can also be found in wooded meadows and in very open deciduous forest. The bashful *N. maculata* has a particularly broad range of habitats that also include pine forests and mossy slopes, often on more or less acid ground. The flowering time of *Neotinea* is mainly spring to early summer, although some populations of *N. ustulata* do not bloom until high or late summer.

Neotinea consistently has a hairless stem, several leaves (most of which are gathered in a basal rosette) and a three-lobed lip with the mid-lobe often being cleft or incised. Its members share many traits with representatives of *Anacamptis* and *Orchis*, but can be recognized by the combination of a dense inflorescence of small to very small flowers, sepals and petals that form a hood over the column and a short-spurred lip without hair tufts.

For many years, only the rather dull-looking *N. maculata* was assigned to this genus. However, recent DNA-based studies clearly suggest that also a few, much prettier, species traditionally assigned to *Orchis* are better classified in *Neotinea*. Now, four species are recognized; they all occur in Europe where *N. tridentata* is even represented by two subspecies. From the Mediterranean region, the British Isles and Central Europe (north to Estonia) the distribution of the genus continues to the Ural Mountains in the north-east and the Caspian Sea in the south-east.

Pollination

No nectar reward is offered to visiting insects, and pollination occurs through generalized food deception – except in the spontaneously self-pollinating *N. maculata*. Whereas the pollinators of *N. lactea* and *N. tridentata* ssp. *conica* remain to be unveiled, the solitary bee, the Red-tailed Mason Bee (*Osmia bicolor*), has been reported as pollinator of *N. tridentata* ssp. *tridentata*.

In *N. ustulata*, the vast majority of populations either bloom in late spring to very early summer or in high to late summer. However, although the divergent flowering times are genetically determined, high rates of gene flow have been demonstrated to occur between the two forms (suggesting an overlap in pollinator fauna). Up to now, the tachinid fly *Tachina magnicornis* and the longhorn beetle *Pseudovadonia livida* have been observed to pollinate early- and late-flowering plants, respectively.

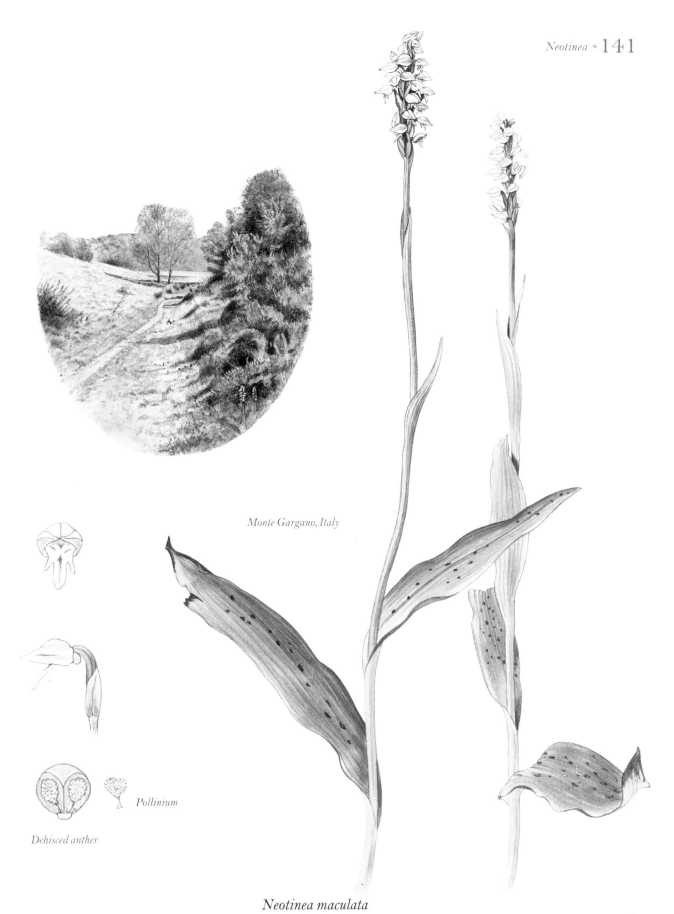

Monte Gargano, Italy

Pollinium

Dehisced anther

Neotinea maculata

DENSE-FLOWERED ORCHID

8–30(–40) cm; spring to early summer; the Mediterranean region, the Canary Islands,
Madeira and the European Atlantic coast north to Ireland.

Öland, Sweden

Neotinea ustulata

BURNT ORCHID

5–50(–80) cm; spring to summer; from western Siberia and the Caspian Sea to most of Europe
(north to Estonia).

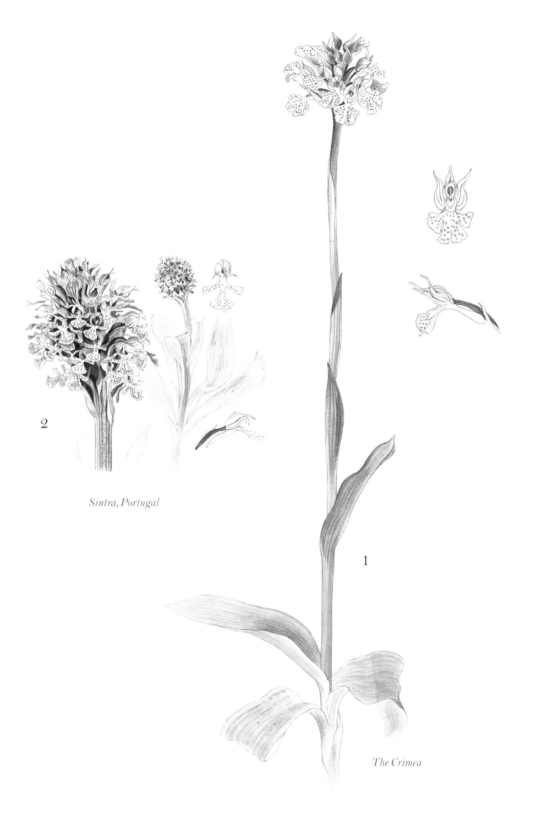

Sintra, Portugal

The Crimea

Neotinea tridentata

TOOTHED ORCHID

pro parte. (1) ssp. *tridentata*; 15–50 cm; spring to summer; south-western Asia, southern Europe (west to France) and central Europe (north to Germany and Poland). (2) ssp. *conica*; 5–30 cm; early spring to early summer; western part of the Mediterranean region (east to north-western Algeria and the Balearic Islands).

San Marino

1

2

Crete

Neotinea tridentata

TOOTHED ORCHID

pro parte (1) ssp. *tridentata*; data given on page 143.

Neotinea lactea

MILKY ORCHID

(2) 5–25 cm; spring; the Mediterranean region
from southern France and north-eastern Algeria
to western Anatolia.

Sketches from Crete

Ophrys

* BEE ORCHIDS *

Sexual lures for male insects

THIS GENUS IS first of all a characteristic element of subtropical vegetation on basic to slightly acid ground – such as garrigue, pine forest, road-side slopes and gaps in deciduous woodland. However, some species also (or exclusively) occur in temperate grassland, fens, hay meadows and open forest on calcareous ground. The flowering time is late winter to summer, with the vast majority of species blooming in spring.

Ophrys is easily recognized by the combination of: (1) bracts that lack conspicuous dark veins and do not envelop the flowers and (2) flowers with a more or less hairy, unspurred lip.

Species delimitation is problematic and eagerly debated; depending on the author, anything between 17 and *c.*350 species may be recognized. Personally, we consider most of the variation to occur below species level, for which reason we only recognize around 20 species (with quite a number of subspecies). The total distribution covers most of Europe, Mediterranean North Africa, Cyprus, the Middle East, the Caucasus and Asia Minor as well as nearby parts of the Near Orient.

Insect pollination

Minute dome-shaped papillae on the margin of the lip and on the apical part of the lower lip surface emit a mixture of scents that specifically attract male insects (mostly belonging to one or other species of solitary bee) through the precise imitation of female sex pheromones (sexually stimulating fragrances). Physical resemblance between the flower and the female insect may contribute to short-distance attraction, but seems to play a more important role in stimulating the male to orient itself longitudinally on the lip. Depending on the *Ophrys* species, the male insect directs either its head or abdomen towards the column and then attempts to copulate with the lip. During this activity it inadvertently deposits or acquires pollinia, or does both (see detailed account of *O. insectifera* ssp. *insectifera* on p. 25).

Self-pollination

The only *Ophrys* species not pollinated by insects is the self-pollinating *O. apifera.* When the flower opens, the anther continues to grow in length, implying that the pollinia are being gradually pulled out; only the viscidia and the extreme base of the stalks remain in place. The stalks are flaccid, so the pollinia gradually tilt downwards until they hang freely in front of the stigma. Aided by a gust of wind, they soon pivot directly onto the stigma.

Öland, Sweden

Ophrys insectifera

FLY ORCHID

(1) ssp. *insectifera*; (5–)10–50(–80) cm; spring to early summer; from England to central Europe –
with extensions to Ireland, Scandinavia, the Moscow region and Mediterranean mountains.
(2) ssp. *aymoninii*; 20–50 cm; late spring to early summer; southern France.

Monte Gargano, Italy

Sintra, Portugal

Ophrys tenthredinifera

SAWFLY OPHRYS

10–30(–45) cm; spring; the Mediterranean region (except its south-easternmost part).

Monte Gargano, Italy

Ophrys bombyliflora

BUMBLEBEE OPHRYS

5–20(–30) cm; spring; the Mediterranean region (except its easternmost part).

Sicily

1

2

3

Ophrys speculum

MIRROR OPHRYS

(1) ssp. *speculum*; 5–25(–30) cm; spring; the Mediterranean region (except its north-easternmost and south-easternmost parts). (2) ssp. *lusitanica*; 15–50 cm; spring; Portugal and southern Spain. (3) ssp. *regis-ferdinandii*; 5–30 cm; spring; the Aegean Islands and neighbouring parts of Anatolia.

Ophrys fusca

DULL OPHRYS

pro parte. (1) ssp. *fusca*; (5–)10–35(–40) cm; late winter to early summer; the Mediterranean region (except its easternmost parts) and western France north to Brittany. (2) ssp. *cinereophila*; 7–25 cm; spring; from Greece to Syria. (3) ssp. *blitopertha*; 7–20 cm; spring; Greece and western Anatolia.

Ophrys fusca

DULL OPHRYS

pro parte. (1) ssp. *iricolor*; 10–40(–70) cm; spring;
scattered in the Mediterranean region. (2) ssp. *pallida*;
10–30 cm; spring; Sicily and north-eastern Algeria.

Ophrys atlantica

ATLAS OPHRYS

(3) 10–30(–35) cm; spring; southern Spain,
northern Morocco and northern Tunisia.

Crete

Ophrys omegaifera

OMEGA OPHRYS

(1) ssp. *omegaifera*; 8–25(–30) cm; late winter to spring; Crete, the Aegean Islands and south-western Anatolia.
(2) ssp. *dyris*; 10–35(–50) cm; spring; from southern Portugal to Mallorca.
(3) ssp. *israelitica*; 8–20(–35) cm; spring; from the Aegean Islands to Israel.
(4) ssp. *fleischmannii*; 8–15(–20) cm; late winter to spring; Crete and the Aegean Islands.
(5) ssp. *hayekii*; 15–22 cm; spring; Sicily and northern Tunisia.

1

Sintra, Portugal

2

3

Ophrys lutea

YELLOW OPHRYS

(1) ssp. *lutea*; 7–30(–40) cm; spring; the Mediterranean region (east to the Aegean Islands) and western France.

(2) ssp. *galilaea*; 5–25 cm; late winter to early summer; the Mediterranean region.

(3) ssp. *melena*; 10–40 cm; spring; Greece and Albania.

Pollinium

Monte Gargano, Italy

Flower in lower front view

Ophrys apifera

BEE ORCHID

(15–)20–50(–70) cm; spring to summer; the Mediterranean and Black Sea regions, western and central Europe
(north to Denmark and southern Sweden).

Southern England

Ophrys apifera

BEE ORCHID

data given on page 155.

Kent, England

Ophrys sphegodes

EARLY SPIDER-ORCHID

pro parte: ssp. *sphegodes*; (10–)15–40(–60) cm; spring to early summer; western, central and southern Europe (north-west to England, south-east to Albania and Corfu).

Ophrys sphegodes

EARLY SPIDER-ORCHID

pro parte. (1) ssp. *sphegodes*; data given on page 157. (2) ssp. *helenae*; 15–40 cm; spring to early summer; Albania and northern Greece.
(3) ssp. *mammosa*; (15–)20–60(–70) cm; spring; from the Balkans to northern Iran and the Caucasus.
(4) ssp. *aesculapii*; 15–40 cm; spring; Greece. (5) ssp. *cretensis*; 20–50 cm; early spring; Crete and the Aegean Islands.
(6) ssp. *passionis*; 20–45 cm; spring; from western France to Italy.

Monte Gargano, Italy

Ophrys sphegodes

EARLY SPIDER-ORCHID

pro parte. (1) ssp. *atrata*; 20–40(–60) cm; spring; southern Europe from Portugal to Albania.
(2) ssp. *sipontensis*; 15–50(–60) cm; spring; south-eastern Italy.

Parnassos, Greece

Ophrys sphegodes

EARLY SPIDER–ORCHID

pro parte: ssp. *spruneri*; (10–)15–40(–50) cm; spring; Greece.

Sicily

Ophrys bertolonii

BERTOLONI'S OPHRYS

10–35 cm; spring to early summer; mainland Italy (south of River Po),
Sicily and the eastern coast of the Adriatic Sea.

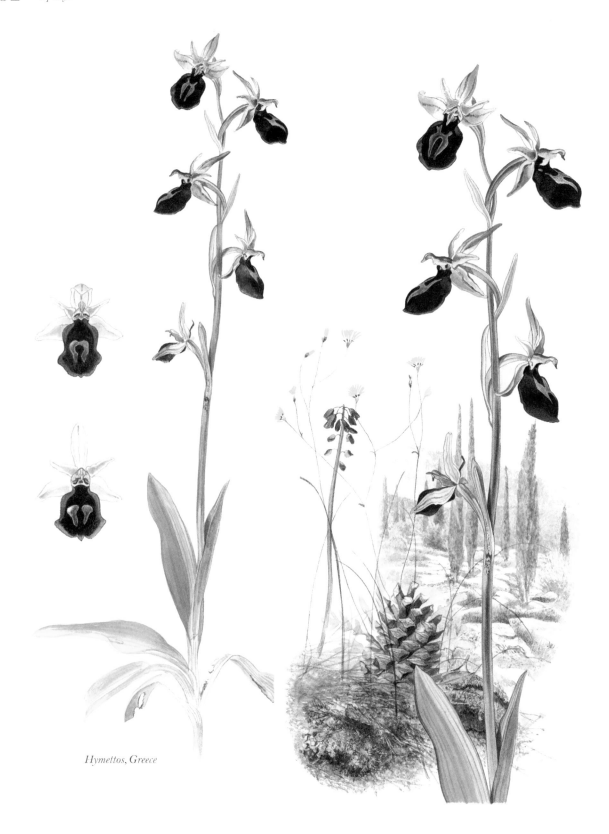

Hymettos, Greece

Ophrys ferrum-equinum ssp. *ferrum-equinum*

HORSESHOE OPHRYS

10–35 cm; spring; from southern Albania across most of Greece to southern Anatolia.

Ophrys argolica

ARGOLIS OPHRYS

(1) ssp. *argolica*; 15–30(–50) cm; spring; the Peloponnese and nearby areas.

(2) ssp. *crabronifera*; 20–65 cm; spring; the Tyrrhenian region of mainland Italy.

(3) ssp. *biscutella*; 10–50(–60) cm; spring; southern mainland Italy and island of Korĉula (Croatia).

(4) ssp. *aegaea*; (7–)10–20(–30) cm; early spring; Karpathos, Kasos and the Cyclades (Greece).

(5) ssp. *lucis*; 10–20(–30) cm; spring; the Dodecanese Islands (Greece) and south-western Anatolia.

1

2

Sparta, Greece

Ophrys reinholdii ssp. *reinholdii*

REINHOLD'S OPHRYS

(1) 15–50 cm; spring; from south-western Anatolia across
most of Greece to adjoining parts of the southern Balkans.

Ophrys lunulata

CRESCENT OPHRYS

(2) 10–40 cm; spring; Sicily.

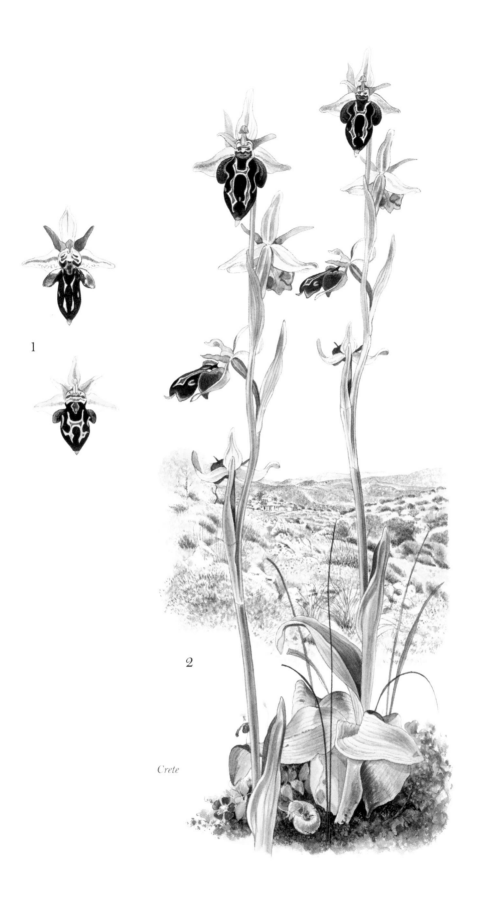

Crete

Ophrys cretica

CRETAN OPHRYS

(1) ssp. *cretica*; 10–40 cm; spring; southern Greece. (2) ssp. *ariadnae*; 10–30 cm; spring; Crete, Karpathos and the Aegean Islands.

Kent, England

Ophrys fuciflora

LATE SPIDER-ORCHID

pro parte. (1) ssp. *fuciflora*; 10–40(–50) cm; spring to summer; from southern England across France and central Europe to the Balkans and the eastern part of the Mediterranean region. (2) ssp. *chestermanii*; 10–30 cm; spring; Sardinia. (3) ssp. *parvimaculata*; 10–35 cm; spring; southern mainland Italy. (4) ssp. *andria*; 15–40(–50) cm; spring; the Cyclades.

Monti Aurunci, Italy

Monte Gargano, Italy

Ophrys fuciflora

LATE SPIDER-ORCHID

pro parte. (1) ssp. *fuciflora*; data given on page 166. (2) ssp. *apulica*; 15–60 cm; spring to early summer; southern Italy.
(3) ssp. *oxyrrhynchos*; 10–30 cm; spring; Malta (extirpated?) and southern Italy. (4) ssp. *lacaitae*; 10–30 cm; late spring
to early summer; Malta (extirpated?), southern Italy and island of Vis (Croatia). (5) ssp. *biancae*; 10–25 cm; spring; Sicily.
(6) ssp. *candica*; 15–45 cm; spring; from southern Italy to south-western Anatolia.

Crete

1

3

2

Southern Spain

Ophrys scolopax

WOODCOCK OPHRYS

pro parte. (1) ssp. *scolopax*; 10–50(–90) cm; spring to early summer; from most of the Mediterranean region to the Caucasus and the Middle East. (2) ssp. *apiformis*; 10–40 cm; spring; south-western part of the Mediterranean region (east to Sicily). (3) ssp. *heldreichii*; 15–45 cm; spring; Greece.

Hymettos, Greece

Ophrys scolopax

WOODCOCK OPHRYS

(1) pro parte: ssp. *cornuta*; 20–50 cm; spring to summer;
from the Caucasus across the Crimea, Anatolia and the
Aegean Islands to south-eastern mainland Europe.

Ophrys umbilicata ssp. *umbilicata*

CARMEL OPHRYS

(2) 10–45(–60) cm; spring; from Albania across Greece and
western/southern Anatolia to Cyprus and Israel.

Steveniella

* HOODED ORCHID *

The 'false-prey syndrome'

STEVENIELLA SATYRIOIDES, the sole species of this genus, requires dry to moist, basic to neutral, fully exposed to partially shaded ground. It is mainly found on grassland and in meadows, open woodland and hazel groves. Flowering occurs from spring to early summer.

Steveniella is easily recognized by the combination of the following features: (1) each flowering shoot bearing only one foliage leaf, placed in a basal position; (2) inflorescence several-flowered; (3) lip hairless, with a partly cleft spur.

The distribution of the genus encompasses northern Anatolia, the Crimea and the Caucasus with neighbouring regions.

Pollination

Steveniella satyrioides is pollinated by workers of social wasps such as *Vespula vulgaris* and *Dolichovespula sylvestris*. Most other plant species pollinated by social wasps offer plenty of freely accessible nectar, but the flowers of *S. satyrioides* lack nectar and are pollinated through deceit. The flowering season is closely synchronized with the establishment of wasp colonies, as the flowers open just around the time when the workers start collecting food for the larvae.

A wasp visiting a *Steveniella* flower assumes a longitudinal position on the lip, inspects the papillae on the basal part of the lip and then inserts its head into the wide spur entrance. Inside the spur, the wasp often scratches the spur wall by its mouthparts. While pressing its head forcefully into the spur, the wasp acquires the pollinia and may efficiently deposit large fragments of previously acquired pollinia on the stigma. In a study population in the Crimea, it was observed that 93 per cent of all flowers were visited and 69 per cent set fruit, implying that the pollination system of *S. satyrioides* is more efficient than those of most other deceptive orchid species.

Social wasps feed their larvae almost exclusively with pulped animal prey, for which reason it has been suggested that the wasps visiting *S. satyrioides* mistake the purple region around the stigma and spur entrance for potential prey. This hypothesis finds some support in observed biting and stinging behaviour of visiting wasps and in the floral scent containing acetophenone, a compound eliciting alarm and attacking behaviour in workers. The deceptive signals of the orchid are termed the 'false-prey syndrome'; a similar system was first observed in the Australian orchid *Calochilus campestris*.

The Crimea

Steveniella satyrioides

HOODED ORCHID

15–60 cm; spring to early summer; from the Crimea to the Caucasus, northern Anatolia and Iran.

Himantoglossum

∗ LIZARD ORCHIDS ∗
Southerners gaining terrain in the north

THE EUROPEAN SPECIES of this genus grow in dry, partially shaded to fully exposed situations on grassland and abandoned agricultural terraces, in scrub, open woodland and garrigue. In general, the plants require basic (to neutral) soil, but *H. metlesicsianum* is restricted to crumbled lava that is weakly acid. Apart from the winter-flowering *H. metlesicsianum* and the consistently spring-flowering *H. robertianum*, all European species bloom from late spring to summer.

In one species of *Himantoglossum* the lip ends in four thread-like processes, and in all other members of the genus the side lobes of the lip have conspicuously wavy margins. None of these features are found in other European orchid genera. It should also be noted that all *Himantoglossum* species are coarse, strong-growing plants and that in most of them the mid-lobe of the lip is extremely elongated and spirally twisted.

This genus, accommodating around 10 species, is distributed in the Middle East, the Mediterranean region (with the Canary Islands) and in adjoining parts of south-central and western Europe, north to England.

Systematics

Until the late 1990s, *H. comperianum* was usually assigned its own genus, *Comperia*, whereas *H. robertianum* and *H. metlesicsianum* were recognized as another separate genus, *Barlia*. However, due to the structural and genetic similarities, most authors now include all these species in a more broadly delimited *Himantoglossum*.

Population growth and dispersal

In this genus, only *H. hircinum* extends from subtropical into temperate regions. Interestingly, the species seems to be expanding in the north, a trend that is particularly well documented in England. Here, the total number of individuals increased from 500 to over 6000 in the period 1988–2000, and the number of populations increased from 10 to 26 in the period 1988–2015. Studies of two British populations have shown that population development is influenced by variation in precipitation and temperature, mainly through effects on fecundity and survival; and, indeed, a sudden rise in the numbers of individuals in the larger British populations coincided with a series of warm, wet winters and hot summers. In turn, the increased average population size led to a marked increase in seed production, which may well have been an important factor for the successful dispersal and founding of new populations.

The Crimea

Himantoglossum comperianum

KOMPER'S ORCHID

25–70 cm; late spring to summer; from the eastern Aegean Islands across Anatolia to the Middle East –
and with isolated occurrences in the Crimea.

1

2

Crete

Himantoglossum metlesicsianum

METLESIC'S ORCHID

(1) 40–60(–110) cm; winter; the Canary Islands.

Himantoglossum robertianum

GIANT ORCHID

(2) 20–80 cm; spring; the Mediterranean region.

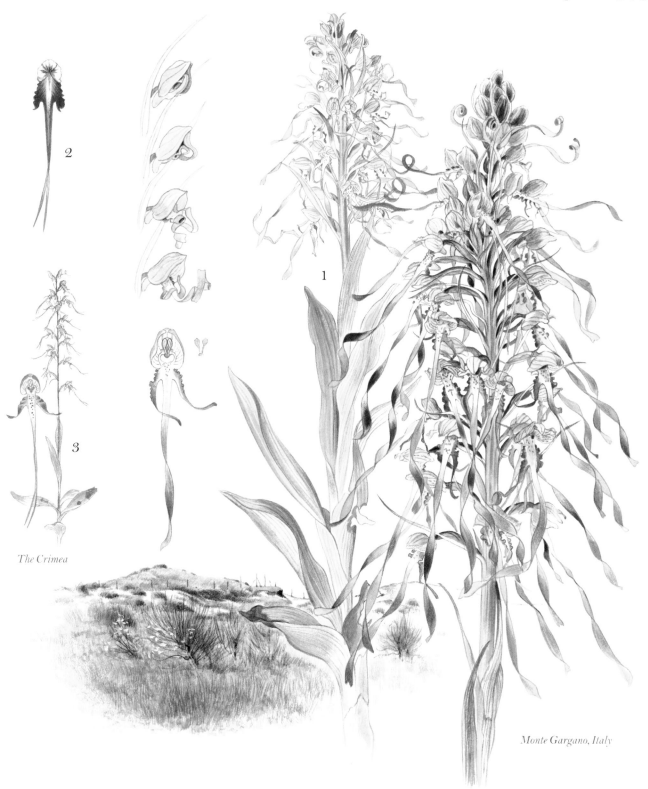

1

2

3

The Crimea

Monte Gargano, Italy

Himantoglossum hircinum

LIZARD ORCHID

(1) 20–90(–110) cm; late spring to summer;
western Mediterranean North Africa and
adjoining parts of Europe (north-east to a line
from England to Bulgaria).

Himantoglossum caprinum

BALKAN LIZARD ORCHID

pro parte (2) ssp. *caprinum*; 25–80(–100) cm; late spring to early
summer; from the eastern Aegean Islands across Anatolia to the
Middle East – and with isolated occurrences in the Crimea.
(3) ssp. *rumelicum*; 35–80 cm; late spring to summer; from
south-eastern Europe across Anatolia to the Caucasus and Palestine.

Serapias

✳ TONGUE-ORCHIDS ✳
Accommodation at a price

S*ERAPIAS* IS A CHARACTERISTIC element in Mediterranean vegetation on basic to slightly acid ground – such as garrigue, road-side slopes, meadows, abandoned agricultural terraces and gaps in deciduous woodland. However, a few species also occur in temperate meadows and grassland. *Serapias* mainly consists of spring-flowering plants, with a couple of species often extending their flowering season to early summer.

Serapias can hardly be mistaken for any other European orchid genus. Particularly characteristic are the large bracts that are subsimilar to the sepals, longitudinally striated by conspicuous dark veins and partly envelope the flowers. It should also be noted that the three-lobed, unspurred lip is more or less hairy in its basal part.

Species delimitation is problematic and debated, but it seems reasonable to estimate that *Serapias* contains around 10 species. The distribution is mainly Mediterranean, but with extensions to the Azores, westernmost Europe, the southern Alps, northern Anatolia and the Caucasus. Casual occurrence of a few species in southern England is often ascribed to deliberate introduction.

Pollination

Serapias parviflora and *S. nurrica* have friable pollinia that soon disintegrate, leading to spontaneous self-pollination; at least in *S. parviflora*, this happens while the flower is still in bud. All other species of the genus are pollinated by insects. As the flowers lack nectar and hardly produce any other consumable pollinator reward (although gnawing of the ridges on the lip base has been occasionally reported), *Serapias* is often claimed to deceive its pollinators. However, this is probably not true as the pollination is conducted by solitary bees (rarely wasps or beetles) that apparently enter the flowers to seek shelter – and the shelter offered by each flower is genuine, implying that the tubular space between the sepals, petals, column and base of the lip constitutes a non-consumable pollinator reward. Thus, the *Serapias* flower offers a shelter that is visited at night and under adverse weather conditions during day-time. However, the bees do not get something for nothing. When a bee creeps head-first into the narrow tubular shelter, it will rub previously acquired pollinia (if any) against the fertile part of the stigma, and it will acquire a new set of pollinia when pushing its head against the liquid-filled pouch containing their common viscidium.

Column

Lip

Pollinia

Column

Monte Gargano, Italy

Recco, Italy

1

2

Serapias cordigera

HEART-FLOWERED SERAPIAS

(1) 8–40(–55) cm; spring to early summer; the Azores,
the Mediterranean region (east to western Anatolia),
Austria and the Atlantic coast of France.

Serapias neglecta ssp. *neglecta*

SCARCE SERAPIAS

(2) 10–30(–35) cm; spring; Sardinia,
Corsica and further north and east to nearby parts of
mainland France and Italy.

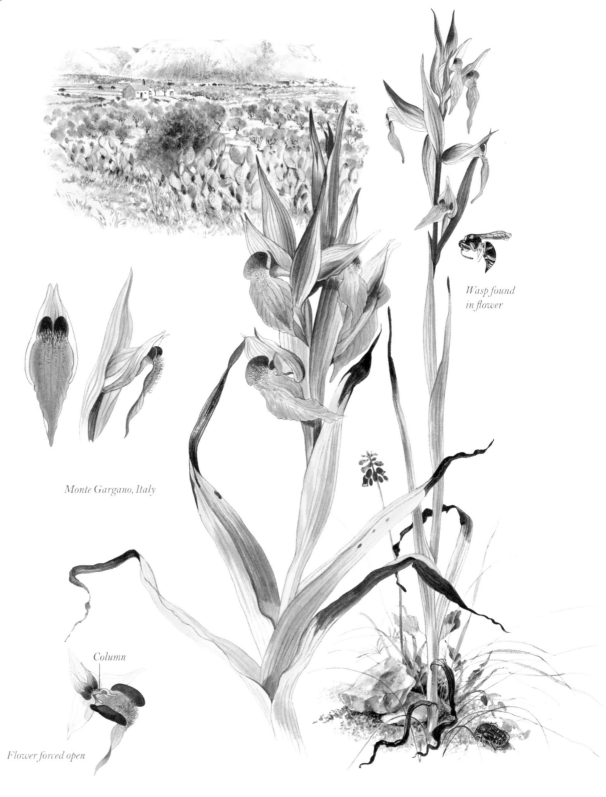

Wasp found in flower

Monte Gargano, Italy

Column

Flower forced open

Serapias vomeracea

PLOUGH–SHARE SERAPIAS

pro parte: ssp. *vomeracea*; 17–60 cm; spring to early summer; the Mediterranean region (east to Greece)
and extending to Switzerland in the north.

1 Crete

2 Monte Gargano, Italy

Serapias vomeracea

PLOUGH–SHARE SERAPIAS

pro parte (1) ssp. *laxiflora*; 15–40(–50) cm; spring; from the Balkans to Anatolia and Cyprus. (2) ssp. *orientalis*; 7–30 cm; spring; from southern Italy to Israel and the western Transcaucasus.

Monte Gargano, Italy

Sicily

Serapias parviflora

SMALL-FLOWERED TONGUE-ORCHID

(1) 10–30(–40) cm; spring; the Canary Islands, the Mediterranean region (east to Cyprus) and the Atlantic coast of France.

Serapias perez-chiscanoi

PEREZ-CHISCANO'S SERAPIAS

(2) 20–40 cm; spring; mainland Portugal and adjoining parts of Spain.

Serapias olbia

HYBRID SERAPIAS

(3) 10–30 cm; spring; south-eastern France.

Monti Aurunci, Italy

1

2

Serapias nurrica	*Serapias lingua*
SARDINIAN SERAPIAS	TONGUE ORCHID
(1) 15–35(–40) cm; spring; Menorca, Corsica, Sardinia, Sicily and Calabria.	(2) 10–35(–50) cm; spring; the Mediterranean region (east to Greece) and major parts of south-western France (north to Brittany).

Anacamptis

TOGETHER, THE EUROPEAN species cover a broad ecological range as they can grow in dry to wet, fertile to fairly poor, basic to slightly acid soil under fully exposed to partially shaded conditions. Depending on the species, typical habitats may include garrigue, scrub, grassland, meadows, fens and woodland. The flowering time is late winter to late summer, with the majority of species flowering in spring or early summer.

Anacamptis consistently has a hairless stem, several leaves and an entire or three-lobed lip with the apical part often being cleft or incised. Its members share many traits with representatives of *Orchis* and *Neotinea*, but can be recognized by the combination of relatively fewer leaves (if any) being assembled in a basal rosette (at least three leaves are usually placed higher up on the stem), an inflorescence of small to fairly large flowers and a lip consistently without tiny tufts of coloured hairs.

Around 10 species are now assigned to *Anacamptis*. The total distribution covers the Mediterranean region and most of Europe (north to the British Isles, southern Scandinavia and Estonia), from where it extends to the Persian Gulf and Kazakhstan.

Systematics and Evolution

For many years, only the butterfly-pollinated *A. pyramidalis* was assigned to this genus. However, recent DNA-based studies indicate that also several (mainly) bee-pollinated species previously assigned to *Orchis* are better classified in *Anacamptis*.

The bee-pollinated species generally have lax inflorescences in which the lip of each individual flower offers a well-defined landing platform for the relatively short-legged bees. Furthermore, the spur is more or less short and broad, implying that it can be efficiently probed by the fairly short mouthparts of a visiting bee. According to the DNA-based studies mentioned above, *A. pyramidalis* has evolved from a bee-pollinated ancestor. The adaptation of *A. pyramidalis* to a different group of pollinators with longer legs and longer and narrower mouthparts has driven the evolution of, for example, a denser inflorescence (enabling a visiting butterfly to place its long legs on more than one flower) and a narrower and longer spur that precisely fits the long and narrow butterfly proboscis. Apart from *A. coriophora* and *A. sancta*, all *Anacamptis* species lack nectar and are pollinated through deceit.

Baia Domizia, Italy

Anacamptis laxiflora ssp. *laxiflora*

LOOSE-FLOWERED ORCHID

(20–)30–60 cm; spring to early summer; from southern Europe and the Crimea to Anatolia,
Cyprus and western Europe (north to the English Channel).

Gotland, Sweden

Anacamptis palustris ssp. *palustris*

SWAMP ORCHID

13–60 cm; spring to summer; northern Tunisia and scattered in most of Europe
(north to the English Channel and Gotland).

Öland, Sweden

Anacamptis pyramidalis

PYRAMIDAL ORCHID

10–60(–80) cm; spring to late summer; south-western Asia, the Mediterranean region
and Europe north to Scotland and Estonia.

Column

Pollinia

Monte Gargano, Italy

Anacamptis pyramidalis

PYRAMIDAL ORCHID

data given on page 185.

Crete

Anacamptis collina

FAN-LIPPED ORCHID

10–50 cm; late winter to spring; scattered from the Mediterranean region to the Middle East.

The Crimea

Anacamptis coriophora

BUG ORCHID

pro parte: ssp. *coriophora*; 15–40(–60) cm; late spring to summer; south-western Asia, the Mediterranean region
and adjoining parts of Europe north to Germany and Estonia (extirpated).

Monte Gargano, Italy

Anacamptis coriophora

BUG ORCHID

pro parte: ssp. *fragrans*; 15–40 cm; spring; from the Mediterranean region to Brittany and to the Middle East.

Column

Pollinia

Rhodes

Anacamptis sancta

HOLY ORCHID

15–40(–50) cm; spring to early summer; eastern Greece, Cyprus and the Mediterranean coast from Anatolia to Israel.

Monti Aurunci, Italy

Anacamptis papilionacea

PINK BUTTERFLY-ORCHID

(1) ssp. *papilionacea*; 15–40(–55) cm; spring; from Corsica and Italy across the Balkans to northern Anatolia.
(2) ssp. *expansa*; 15–40(–55) cm; spring; western part of the Mediterranean region (east to Sicily and southern mainland Italy).

Crete

Anacamptis boryi

BORY'S ORCHID

10–35(–45) cm; spring; Greece (mainly Crete and the Peloponnese).

Öland, Sweden

Anacamptis morio

GREEN-WINGED ORCHID

pro parte: ssp. *morio*; (4–)7–30(–50) cm; spring to early summer;
most of Europe north to Scotland, southern Scandinavia and Estonia.

Sicily

Anacamptis morio

GREEN-WINGED ORCHID

pro parte: ssp. *longicornu*; 10–35 cm; spring; the Balearic Islands, Corsica, Sardinia,
Sicily, northern Tunisia and northern Algeria.

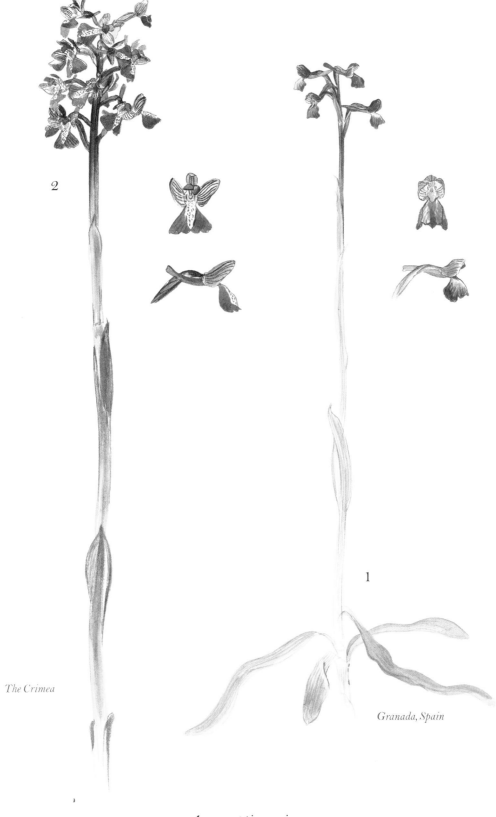

The Crimea

Granada, Spain

Anacamptis morio

GREEN-WINGED ORCHID

pro parte. (1) ssp. *champagneuxii*; 10–25(–40) cm; spring to early summer; from southern France across
the Iberian Peninsula to Morocco and north-western Algeria.
(2) ssp. *caucasica*; 12–30 cm; spring to early summer; south-eastern Europe and south-western Asia.

How to learn more

Orchid identification

YOU SHOULD BE ABLE to identify most European orchids (on the spot) by matching the plants you find with watercolours in this book. However, a few rare species, subspecies and varieties are not included here. In due course, you might consider supplementing this book with one or more photographic field guides, in which you may also find descriptions and identification keys.

Whenever possible, identification should be based on fresh, healthy and fully developed individuals. Furthermore, floral features should be examined in flowers in the mid-portion of the inflorescence, as flowers situated in the upper or lower end may be less typical.

Sometimes, you will encounter an orchid that is not easy to identify. In many such cases, you will be looking at either a less typical individual, an aberrant form, a fortuitous hybrid or a member of a hybrid swarm or partly stabilized hybrid complex (see below).

Variation

For most species (not to speak of subspecies or varieties) it requires a certain degree of experience before you can identify them correctly on every encounter. This is mainly because many species vary considerably.

Problems mainly arise when two or more species of the same genus occur together. In such cases, it is a good strategy first to get an impression of how many groups of largely similar individuals can be distinguished at the site. Next, you should select a few representative plants of one group at a time and try to identify them. Examining more than one individual at a time reduces the risk of one aberrant feature in one individual leading to misidentification – but it is obviously of crucial importance that the individuals examined together actually belong to one and the same species!

Aberrant forms

Now and then, aberrant forms are encountered, usually as solitary individuals. Due to a small genetic change, one or a few organs look completely different from what is the normal condition in the species. You should suspect that you are looking at an aberrant form if, for example, your plant has: (1) white to rose-coloured leaves; (2) a petal-like lip; (3) lip-like lateral petals; (4) flowers of an extremely deep purple colour; or (5) white or very pale yellowish-green flowers.

Fortuitous hybrids

Hybrids usually look more or less intermediary between the parental (sub)species. However, many non-hybrids have been misidentified as hybrids, simply because one unusual feature (for example, rose-coloured flowers in a normally purple-flowered species) happens to match the normal condition in a related species. A plant should be suspected to be a hybrid mainly if it shows intermediacy

Variation in
Dactylorhiza incarnata
var. *incarnata*,
exemplified by three
individuals from
Öland, Sweden

in several individual characters – each of which otherwise tends to separate two species occurring at the same site.

Still, it is difficult (sometimes even impossible) to positively identify hybrids, as both hybrids and parental species can be highly variable. However, by spending a lot of time examining orchids in the field, you can gradually become fairly skilled at recognizing fortuitous hybrids.

Fortuitous hybrids between *Dactylorhiza incarnata* var. *incarnata* and *D. maculata* ssp. *fuchsii.* Öland, Sweden

Hybrid swarms

Hybrids may be fully fertile, especially if formed between closely related species (or between different subspecies of the same species). In such cases, second- and higher-generation hybrids can be produced, and back-crossing to either parental species may also result in fertile progeny. Thus, after just a few generations, an almost continuous range of forms may span the original genetic gap between the two parental species. Such an aggregation of plants is called a hybrid swarm, and the visually recognizable variation is no less complex than the genetic relationships. In reality, it is impossible to identify most of the individual plants. If you are lucky, you can still find some typical individuals of the parental species at the site, but you have to accept that the rest are simply members of the hybrid swarm.

Partly stabilized hybrid complexes

At least in the genus *Ophrys*, there seems to be a number of cases (though not thoroughly documented) in which the fertile hybrid between two species turns out to be competitive in a certain region, which sometimes extends beyond the geographic range of either parental species. Such plants evidently are more or less self-contained evolutionary entities, and they are probably best referred to as partly stabilized hybrid complexes.

To the orchid enthusiast, they would typically make the impression of highly variable species. One example is the so-called *Ophrys × arachnitiformis*, which is presumably a hybrid complex between *O. fuciflora* and *O. sphegodes*. The cross in front of the specific epithet indicates that we are dealing with a plant of hybrid nature rather than a true species.

Ophrys fuciflora ssp. *fuciflora*

Ophrys sphegodes ssp. *sphegodes*

Flowers illustrating variation in *Ophrys × arachnitiformis*

Orchid tourism

No MATTER WHICH European country you live in, and no matter in which part of that country you live, you should be able to encounter native orchids in your close surroundings. However, some areas are much richer in orchids than others, and no single region in Europe accommodates all the orchid species native to that continent. Therefore, even if your local area is rich in orchids, you eventually will be tempted to travel to find more. Orchid tourism can be practiced all the year round, but with the majority of species to be found in bloom within the period from March until August.

Preparations

To make an orchid trip successful, it is crucial that you plan it thoroughly. First of all, you should choose the destination based on which species you would particularly like to find. The same goes for the timing of your trip, as nearly all European orchid species only bloom for a few weeks a year, and as the flowering time of individual species may vary with latitude and altitude.

Distributions and flowering times of all species and subspecies included in this book are given at the bottom of each colour plate; but this information is only sufficient for rough overall planning. You can obtain more detailed information from excursion reports and papers on local orchid floras published in orchid journals; and experienced members of orchid societies are usually happy to share their knowledge and notes with novices. In this context, the online discussion forums offered by several societies (see p. 204) can be useful tools for establishing fruitful contacts.

Logistics also have to be considered before you go abroad; for example, detailed maps are useful, and a rented vehicle may greatly widen your possibilities during the trip.

Where to go

A few orchid species only occur in a very small part of Europe. This is true for the few endemic species (see p. 30), but also a number of species with wide total ranges that only reach one or another small corner of Europe. The latter species include, for example, *Spiranthes romanzoffiana* (western part of the British Isles), *Platanthera hyperborea* (Iceland), *Ophrys atlantica* (southernmost Spain) and *Steveniella satyrioides* (the Crimea). Thus, if you are determined to find all the species and subspecies of European orchids in the wild, you will need to visit major parts of the continent. However, most orchid enthusiasts primarily want to visit areas with a wide range of species – and preferably with some of them occurring abundantly.

Jalta in the Crimea, the Ukraine ›

KRIM/JALTA 26/X 1978 (FRÅN HOTELL ORLANDA)   Jan Martin 1978

Societies and journals

Sooner or later you will probably start feeling a need to share your growing orchid interest with others, to be continuously updated with new information and to regularly consult more experienced people in this field. All the needs can be met by joining one or more societies. Nearly all relevant societies organize meetings, lectures and excursions, publish a journal, and an increasing number offer online discussion forums.

Generalist societies

Membership of a botanical society (or natural history society), such as the Botanical Society of Britain & Ireland (BSBI), is ideal if you want to explore European orchids in an ecologically and systematically broader perspective. In addition, it is often possible to join or establish an orchid study group within the framework of a society of this kind. A number of such groups exist, for example Section Orchidées d'Europe (under Naturalistes Belges) and Werkgroep Europese Orchideeën (under Koninklijke Nederlandse Natuurhistorische Vereniging).

General orchid societies, such as the Orchid Society of Great Britain, likewise exist in most countries. They are usually dominated by orchid growers and primarily focus on tropical orchids. They are recommended to people who have developed an interest in European orchids, but wish to expand their curiosity to the higher structural, ecological and systematic diversity of orchids from the tropics. Membership of a general orchid society is particularly rewarding to those who find as much pleasure in growing orchids at home as studying them in their natural environment.

Specialist societies

Ten individual orchid study groups exist in Germany. They primarily serve to promote conservation of the local orchid species and their habitats. However, a wider interest in European and Mediterranean orchids also thrives in the study groups, as reflected by the content of their journals: Journal Europäischer Orchideen (published by Arbeitskreis Heimische Orchideen Baden-Württenberg) and Berichte aus den Arbeitskreisen Heimische Orchideen (published by the nine remaining groups).

A number of societies reminiscent of the German study groups are found across Europe. Their websites, journals, online forums and so on are predominantly in the native languages. Two of the most active specialist societies are the Hardy Orchid Society (Britain; publishes the Journal of the Hardy Orchid Society) and Gruppo Italiano Ricerca Orchidee Spontanee (publishes the journal Orchidee Spontanee d'Europa).

INDEX TO EXPLANATIONS OF SPECIAL TERMS